MW00878852

Wisdom's Seven Pillars

WISDOM'S SEVEN PILLARS

By Nancy Sari

XULON PRESS

Xulon Press
2301 Lucien Way #415
Maitland, FL 32751
407.339.4217
www.xulonpress.com

© 2020 by Nancy Sari

All rights reserved solely by the author. The author
guarantees all contents are original and do not infringe upon
the legal rights of any other person or work. No part of this
book may be reproduced in any form without the permission
of the author. The views expressed in this book are not
necessarily those of the publisher.

Unless otherwise indicated, Scripture quotations taken from
the King James Version (KJV)–*public domain*.

Printed in the United States of America.

ISBN-13: 978-1-6305-0278-2

Table of Contents

Introduction ix

Dedication. xi

Acknowledgements xiii

Wisdom's House xv

Pillar #1: Fear of the LORD 1

The Fear of the LORD Is to Hate Pride 2

The Fear of the LORD Is to Hate Arrogancy . . . 20

The Fear of the LORD Is to Hate the Evil Way . . 28

The Fear of the LORD Is to Hate the

      Froward Mouth. 44

Further Study for Fear of the LORD 54

Pillar #2: Instruction **57**

Receiving Instruction. 59

Refusing Instruction 68

Further Study for Instruction 70

Pillar #3: Knowledge **73**

Knowledge of God 73

Knowledge of Man 81

Knowledge of Sin 90

Knowledge of God's Word. 100

Lack of Knowledge. 111

Further Study for Knowledge 114

Pillar #4: Understanding **117**

Understanding and Talents 118

Understanding and Timing 123

Understanding and Tantrums 129

Understanding and Treasure 132

Further Study for Understanding 135

Pillar #5: Discretion **137**

Beware of the False Friend 139

Beware of the Fool 143

Beware of the Flatterer 148

Discretion and Potiphar's Wife 151

Further Study for Discretion 167

Pillar #6: Counsel **169**

Seek the LORD 172

Agree with God's Word 178

Trust in the LORD 182

Receive His Promise 188

Further Study for Counsel 191

Pillar #7: Reproof **193**

   Confrontation 194

   Correction 200

   Restitution 209

   Further Study for Reproof 212

Answer Keys for Further Study Sections 213

Notes 221

About the Author 227

Introduction

Years ago, at a ladies' luncheon, I gave a talk entitled *Welcome the Word,* in which I used Proverbs 9:1–6 as my text. As I prepared for the luncheon, I kept wondering what the seven pillars were in Proverbs 9:1. I decided to find out. Through prayer and Bible study, God revealed the seven pillars. What began as a search to satisfy my own interest became this Bible study.

Each pillar has taught me valuable lessons. The order of the pillars is important since Scripture says that wisdom has a beginning, and that beginning is the pillar Fear of the LORD. Each pillar after that is supported by the previous one until all seven are in place. Reproof is the final pillar because God uses it to guide us back to the other pillars and reminds us that we are His children.

May God use these lessons in your life for His glory and your good.

Dedication

To my sister in the Lord, Sharon Revello,
a friend forever

Acknowledgements

From studying, to writing, to getting published, I have several people to thank for this Bible study. My husband Anthony shared his study materials, answered questions, and gave me time to get this finished.

Marcia Jansson, my aunt, greatly encouraged me to complete this study and suggested the "Further Study" section.

My dear sister in the Lord, Sharon Revello, offered constructive comments and proofread most of it. Her comment "Wow—could not put it down," is probably the greatest compliment a writer could receive. She was also my prayer warrior. God answering prayer got this book published. The staff at Xulon Press were encouraging and helpful from the first phone call. Whatever eternal rewards there may be because of this book, each of you will have a share.

Most of all, I thank my heavenly Father who provided all that was needed to get this study into print. All glory to God!

Wisdom's House

———— ✝ ————

When we think about a place to live, what comes to mind? A brick house, a log cabin, a furnished apartment, or a camper are all possibilities. When considering Wisdom's house, what image appears? Scripture suggests a building with pillars, much like a temple would have. *Wisdom hath builded her house, she hath hewn out her seven pillars* (Proverbs 9:1).

Wisdom's house is unique. Anyone can choose to live there. It will last forever, and all who live there are blessed. Her house is built on a solid foundation—the Rock. "Who is the Rock?" you ask. Moses testified of Him and said to hear his words,

> *Because I will publish the name of the LORD: ascribe ye greatness unto our God. He is the Rock, his work is perfect: for all*

his ways are judgment: a God of truth and without iniquity, just and right is he (Deuteronomy 32:3–4).

Because Wisdom's house is built on the Rock, it can withstand any amount of rainfall, floods, and wind storms. Jesus said,

Therefore whosoever heareth these sayings of mine, and doeth them, I will liken him unto a wise man, which built his house upon a rock: And the rain descended, and the floods came, and the winds blew, and beat upon that house; and it fell not: for it was founded upon a rock (Matthew 7:24–25).

The rain is the everyday temptations and troubles. For example, we may be tempted to be selfish, neglect a responsibility, or complain about having leftovers. Troubles may include a car nicknamed Old Unfaithful or cleaning up spills at nearly every meal. Wisdom's house stands in the rainfall of daily temptations and troubles. The floods are the overwhelming trials. We are in danger of being swept away by man's philosophies, sin, or waves of uncontrolled emotions. Wisdom's house stands against the floods that threaten to damage and destroy us. The winds are words that attack us. They may be lies, criticism, gossip, or ridicule. Wisdom's house stands against the powerful winds of hateful, hurtful words. Just as the hymn *A Shelter in the Time of Storm* reminds us, we have a place of refuge amidst the raging storms of life.

Upon the foundation of that refuge, Wisdom has carved out seven pillars to uphold her abode—pillars that will uphold us as well. These pillars are: Fear of the LORD, Instruction, Knowledge, Understanding, Discretion, Counsel, and Reproof.

Author's Note: A Bible verse is given with each pillar. This may be used as a memory verse.

Pillar #1

Fear of the LORD

The fear of the LORD is the beginning of wisdom: and the knowledge of the holy is understanding (Proverbs 9:10).

F ear of the LORD is the central pillar of Wisdom's house because it is the beginning of wisdom, and the other pillars could not stand without it. For example, the pillars of Instruction and Knowledge are established by Fear of the LORD.

The fear of the LORD is the instruction of wisdom (Proverbs 15:33a).

The fear of the LORD is the beginning of knowledge (Proverbs 1:7a).

Scripture defines Fear of the LORD in Proverbs 8:13 as, *The fear of the LORD is to hate evil: pride, and arrogancy, and the evil way, and the froward mouth, do I hate.* The word *hate*[1] in this verse comes from the Hebrew word "sane" (saw-nay') meaning "to personally hate as an enemy or foe." Here we learn that our enemies are Pride, Arrogancy, the Evil Way, and the Froward Mouth.

The Fear of the LORD Is to Hate Pride

Pride is evil. It's the sin that corrupted the archangel Lucifer and will corrupt us. God made Lucifer to be full of wisdom and perfect in beauty; he was the musical cherub of heaven.

> *Son of man, take up a lamentation upon the king of Tyrus, and say unto him, Thus saith the Lord GOD; Thou sealest up the sum, full of wisdom, and perfect in beauty. Thou hast been in Eden the garden of God; every precious stone was thy covering, the sardius, topaz, and the diamond, the beryl, the onyx, and the jasper, the sapphire, the emerald, and the carbuncle, and gold: the workmanship of thy tabrets and of thy*

pipes was prepared in thee in the day that thou wast created. Thou art the anointed cherub that covereth; and I have set thee so: thou wast upon the holy mountain of God; thou hast walked up and down in the midst of the stones of fire. Thou wast perfect in thy ways from the day that thou wast created, till iniquity was found in thee (Ezekiel 28:12–15).

Lucifer took his eyes off God, looked at himself, and whistled. His gem stones glittered, and his tabrets and pipes were a perfect fit. He was beautiful; he was bright. Admiring himself was his downfall; it corrupted his wisdom.

Thine heart was lifted up because of thy beauty, thou hast corrupted thy wisdom by reason of thy brightness (Ezekiel 28:17a).

Most of us wouldn't admit to admiring ourselves at times, but we do. God created beauty, so there's nothing wrong with being beautiful. The problem comes when we take our eyes off God and think we are the greatest. It's the mentality: If you're looking for the best, look at me. Pride then moves self onto the throne, making self to be equal with God.

As Pride welled up in Lucifer, he felt worthy of God's throne.

> *For thou hast said in thine heart, I will ascend into heaven, I will exalt my throne above the stars of God: I will sit also upon the mount of the congregation, in the sides of the north: I will ascend above the heights of the clouds; I will be like the most High (Isaiah 14:13–14).*

Lucifer exalted himself, and God cast him out of heaven. He lost all he had. *How art thou fallen from heaven, O Lucifer, son of the morning! how art thou cut down to the ground, which didst weaken the nations* (Isaiah 14:12)*!* When we exalt ourselves, get ready, because destruction is coming. *Pride cometh before destruction, and an haughty spirit before a fall* (Proverbs 16:18).

Pride expects to be the one always chosen. Pride says, "I am the one. It's up to me." Looking at things realistically, I may not be the one God will use right now. I am not the only vessel on God's table. It is right to be willing to be used, but God will choose which vessel He wants. *But in a great house there are not only vessels of gold and silver, but also of wood and of earth; and some to honour, and some to dishonour* (II Timothy 2:20). This verse reminds us that there are different vessels for various purposes. Pride would consider herself a vessel of gold or silver, someone to honor, and expects to be the one always used and not left on the table. We see this when one choir member was asked to sing a solo, and "Miss Golden Voice" was not asked. Miss Golden Voice was not happy and made sure others knew she was not happy.

Pride reveals herself in demanding attention, applause, and awards. To get attention, Pride will arrive late—on purpose—to make a grand entrance. All eyes must be on her. She will also talk and talk and talk and talk and talk. All ears must listen to her. As Pride wants to be heard, she gets louder and louder. In musical terms, Pride is building toward a crescendo.

Getting louder can mean that Pride is becoming angry. Anger is probably the emotion most associated with Pride. A loud, angry outburst certainly gets attention. However, wanting attention for our own glory brings shame. Consider Miriam, the sister of Aaron and Moses. She gave glory to God when He destroyed the Egyptian army in the Red Sea.

> *And Miriam the prophetess, the sister of Aaron, took a timbrel in her hand; and all the women went out after her with timbrels and with dances. And Miriam answered them, Sing ye to the LORD, for he hath triumphed gloriously; the horse and his rider hath he thrown into the sea (Exodus 15:20–21).*

Notice that she was center stage yet praising the Lord; she did not demand attention. After a year or so passed, Miriam and Aaron had this conversation:

> *And Miriam and Aaron spake against Moses because of the Ethiopian woman whom he had married: for he had married an Ethiopian woman. And they said, Hath the LORD indeed spoken only by Moses?*

hath he not spoken also by us? And the LORD heard it (Numbers 12:1–2).

This is a good reminder that God hears our conversations. God heard they were making themselves equal with Moses. They both held positions of leadership; Miriam was a prophetess and Aaron was the high priest, but God spoke to Moses face to face, not in visions or dreams.

And the LORD came down in the pillar of the cloud, and stood in the door of the tabernacle, and called Aaron and Miriam: and they both came forth. And he said, Hear now my words: If there be a prophet among you, I the LORD will make myself known unto him in a vision, and will speak unto him in a dream. My servant Moses is not so, who is faithful in all mine house. With him will I speak mouth to mouth, even apparently, and not in dark speeches; and the similitude of the LORD shall he behold: wherefore then were ye not afraid to speak against my servant Moses? And the anger of the LORD was kindled against them; and he departed (Numbers 12:5–9).

Pride entered Miriam's heart when she wanted center stage for herself, and she got the attention of the entire camp.

> And the cloud departed from off the tabernacle; and, behold, Miriam became leprous, white as snow: and Aaron looked upon Miriam, and, behold, she was leprous. [...] And the LORD said unto Moses, If her father had but spit in her face, should she not be ashamed seven days? let her be shut out from the camp seven days, and after that let her be received in again. And Miriam was shut out from the camp seven days: and the people journeyed not till Miriam was brought in again (Numbers 12:10,14–15).

Miriam's neighbor: "Did you hear about Miriam?"

Woman in the camp: "Miriam the prophetess?"

Miriam's neighbor: "Yes, she has leprosy! We have to stay here in Hazeroth for seven days until she is brought back into camp."

Woman in the camp: "It's shameful. Just think, we women once followed her."

Consider what happened to Miriam because of Pride; she ended up in shame. Proverbs 11:2 warns, *When pride cometh, then cometh shame: but with the lowly is wisdom.*

Applause is another demand of Pride. Consider the following scenario:

"Mommy, I'm hungry. Will you make me a sandwich?"

"Ask somebody else. I have to get a meal to the new family in the neighborhood. You know we need to show them Christian love. Now help me carry this food to the car."

She then reports at church that she brought a meal to the new family and invited them to church. The church responds with applause.

What's the problem? She ignored her own child because there would be no applause for making Johnny a sandwich. Pride expects recognition and congratulations for her deeds. Otherwise, she whines, "No one appreciates all I do."

In the early church, Barnabas was willing and able to give a donation to the church to help the needy.

> *Neither was there any among them that lacked: for as many as were possessors of lands or houses sold them, and brought the prices of the things that were sold, And laid them down at the apostles' feet: and distribution was made unto every man according as he had need. And Joses, who by the apostles was surnamed Barnabas, (which is, being interpreted, The son of consolation,) a Levite, and of the country of Cyprus, Having land, sold it, and brought the money, and laid it at the apostles' feet (Acts 4:34–37).*

There was a husband and wife in the same church, and they wanted to do the same thing. They sold land, kept back part of the price, which was fine, but then they said to the apostles that they were giving all the money like Barnabas had. When the husband presented the money, he was expecting applause.

But Peter said, Ananias, why hath Satan filled thine heart to lie to the Holy Ghost, and to keep back part of the price of the land? Whiles it remained, was it not thine own? and after it was sold, was it not in thine own power? why hast thou conceived this thing in thine heart? thou hast not lied unto men, but unto God (Acts 5:3–4).

God's judgment came swift and sure. *And Ananias hearing these words fell down, and gave up the ghost: and great fear came on all them that heard these things* (Acts 5:5). Later that same day, Sapphira came to see Peter. God's mercy gave Sapphira the opportunity to tell the truth.

And Peter answered unto her, Tell me whether ye sold the land for so much? And she said, Yea, for so much. Then Peter said unto her, How is it that ye have agreed together to tempt the Spirit of the Lord? behold, the feet of them which have buried thy husband are at the door, and shall carry thee out. Then she fell down straightway at his feet, and yielded up the ghost: and the young men came in, and

> *found her dead, and, carrying her forth,*
> *buried her by her husband. (Acts 5:8–10).*

Their desire for applause was greater than their desire for truth, and it cost them their lives.

Pride will elicit applause. *Elicit*[2] comes from the Latin "e" (out) + "lacere" (to deceive), hence to draw out by deceit. By not telling the whole truth, Pride will deceive others into applauding.

Pride: I entered a local holiday cooking contest, and I won two first place prizes and one second place prize. All three of my recipes were featured in the newspaper. (Of course, all applaud.)

Truth: Years ago, the local newspaper in Keokuk, Iowa, held a holiday cooking contest just before Thanksgiving. On the day of the contest, I rushed three holiday side dishes and two of my children to the newspaper office. We arrived ten minutes late and were disheveled. I was afraid that we were too late for the judging. Instead, we were loudly and warmly greeted by the two newspaper employees and the only other contestant. She, too, had entered three dishes. The six of us, my children included, sampled and voted for each dish. Of course, I won two first place prizes and one second place prize; my children and I cast half the votes! My prizes totaled one hundred dollars' worth of gift certificates from local businesses. Thrilled and thankful, I used the certificates to buy Christmas gifts. All six recipes were printed in the newspaper. That is what really happened.

Pride may receive applause until the whole truth is known. Then Pride is wounded by her own words. *Bread of deceit is sweet to a man; but afterwards his mouth shall be filled with gravel* (Proverbs 20:17).

Pride demands awards: certificates, plaques, and trophies are evidence that she is great. Receiving awards is not the problem; boasting about awards is the problem. "See my award? I certainly deserved it." Pride wants all the credit for the accomplishment and forgets that others have helped make it happen. At the end of baseball season, no one makes it to the World Series alone. Unlike Pride, thank others, then cheer for the trophy, rejoice in achieving a blue ribbon and hang up that recognition plaque, but don't boast about it. Shout a hearty "Thank you, Lord!" and give praise where it is due.

Pride thinks she has all the answers in life and gets angry if you do not accept her answer. For example, health and wellness is big business today. My husband and I had been involved with a company in that industry. Because of it, we have met several people who sell products that offer "better health and more wealth."

Seriously there is no such thing as a miracle herb. If we have poor eating habits, drink alcohol, smoke, exercise very little, and ignore doctor's instructions, then no amount of anything will make us strong and healthy. There are also certain conditions God allows someone to endure for His glory and the person's good. Consider Paul for example. God didn't want Paul lifted up with Pride, so he was given a thorn in the flesh. *And lest I should be exalted above measure through the abundance of the revelations, there was given to me a thorn in the flesh, the messenger of Satan to buffet me, lest I should be exalted above measure* (II Corinthians 12:7). God's strength would be revealed through Paul's weakness.

> *For this thing I besought the Lord thrice,*
> *that it might depart from me. And he said*
> *unto me, My grace is sufficient for thee: for*

my strength is made perfect in weakness.
Most gladly therefore will I rather glory
in my infirmities, that the power of Christ
may rest upon me (II Corinthians 12:8–9).

Pride will not accept weakness for God's glory. Pride believes she is the expert and is convinced she can help everyone with what she knows. My husband and I met a woman like that a while ago. She became angry when I looked at the supplements she was selling and refused them. They were the typical assortment, and I already knew supplements were not the answer to my husband's health issues. The woman's Pride could not accept, "No, thank you."

Pride does not seek God. *The wicked, through the pride of his countenance, will not seek after God: God is not in all his thoughts* (Psalm 10:4). The wicked refuse to acknowledge God.

Consider the evolutionist. The idea of evolution is to eliminate God as the Creator. The precise design and intricacy of nature and the universe clearly show a Creator, yet evolutionists deny His existence. *For the invisible things of him from the*

creation of the world are clearly seen, being under-
stood by the things that are made, even his eternal
power and Godhead; so that they are without excuse
(Romans 1:20). Evolutionist Sir Arthur Keith
admitted, "Evolution is unproved and unprovable.
We believe it only because the only alternative is
special creation, and that is unthinkable."[3] Dr. Karl
Popper stated, "Evolution is not a fact. Evolution
does not even qualify as a theory or as a hypoth-
esis. It is a metaphysical [abstract] research pro-
gram and it is not really testable science."[4]

The atheist claims there is no God, but God says,
The fool hath said in his heart, There is no God. They
are corrupt, they have done abominable works, there
is none that doeth good (Psalm 14:1). Atheists do no
good. They do not care for orphans or widows. Has
an atheist encouraged adoption instead of abortion? Do they reach out to the poor and needy?

Pride can also cause God's people to not have Him
in their thoughts.

> *They provoked him to jealousy with*
> *strange gods, with abominations pro-*
> *voked they him to anger. They sacrificed*

unto devils, not to God; to gods whom they knew not, to new gods that came newly up, whom your fathers feared not. Of the Rock that begat thee thou art unmindful, and hast forgotten God that formed thee (Deuteronomy 32:16–18).

What has taken the place of God in our thoughts? God's people are looking to Eastern mysticism practices, such as yoga, to find peace. The source of peace is not our sinful selves; it comes from God. Quiet time is of great benefit if we are seeking God. Scripture states:

Be still, and know that I am God: I will be exalted among the heathen, I will be exalted in the earth (Psalm 46:10).

My meditation of him shall be sweet: I will be glad in the LORD (Psalm 104:34).

Pride opposes God's Word.

God's Word	Pride
For all have sinned, and come short of the glory of God (Romans 3:23).	I'm really a good person; God will accept me.
Wives, submit yourselves unto your own husbands, as unto the Lord (Ephesians 5:22).	I know what to do better than my husband does.
And when ye stand praying, forgive, if ye have ought against any: that your Father also which is in heaven may forgive you your trespasses (Mark 11:25).	You don't understand; I have been hurt. They aren't even sorry!
My help cometh from the LORD, which made heaven and earth (Psalm 121:2).	I can handle this; I am a strong person.

The list goes on. This is the greatest battle of the will. Will I obey God's Word or my Pride?

Only by pride cometh contention: but with the well advised is wisdom (Proverbs 13:10). Paul and Barnabas had served together as God's chosen missionary team, yet they were parted because of contention. Their argument would have sounded familiar.

Barnabas: "We should take John Mark with us."

Paul: 'No, we shouldn't."

Barnabas: 'Yes, we should."

Paul: 'No, we won't!"

Barnabas: "Yes, we will!'

Paul: "NO!"

Barnabas: "YES!"

Paul: "If he comes, I won't go."

Barnabas: "Fine with me."

Scripture says the following regarding their disagreement:

> *And the contention was so sharp between them, that they departed asunder one from*

the other: and so Barnabas took Mark, and sailed unto Cyprus; And Paul chose Silas, and departed, being recommended by the brethren unto the grace of God (Acts 15:39–40).

It would have made a difference if they had agreed to pray, or even fast and pray, about taking John Mark. God knew whether John Mark should have joined them on that missionary journey or not. Pride leaves God out of our thinking. *The beginning of strife is as when one letteth out water: therefore leave off contention, before it be meddled with* (Proverbs 17:14). We may win an argument and maintain Pride, but we lose far more. Pride has destroyed marriages, sibling relationships, friendships, and even ministries.

Pride is our greatest foe. It can overcome us anywhere and anytime. We hate Pride in others, and we must recognize and defeat Pride in ourselves.

The Fear of the LORD Is to Hate Arrogancy

Arrogancy is evil. Pride and Arrogancy are two sides of the same coin—the coin of self. Webster's dictionary defines *Arrogancy*[5] as "a sense of supe-riority which manifests itself in an overbearing manner; presumption in claiming rank, dignity, or power." Arrogancy is the root cause for someone to excuse herself for breaking rules and disobeying laws but expects others to obey them. This person will say, "I have a good reason for why the rule doesn't apply to me."

Arrogancy thinks she is among the elite who are above menial tasks. "I don't wash out trash cans." Her superior attitude keeps her at a distance from those she deems unworthy of her attention. "I wouldn't waste time on them." Arrogancy will help someone else but often puts down the one being helped. "If you weren't such an idiot, you would know how to do this yourself." (To help us idiots, there are books like *Idiot's Guide: Calculus I*. Wasn't he a Roman emperor?)

Arrogancy thinks of her schedule above the needs of others. After all, she is more important than anyone else. How do we respond to daily interrup-tions? I am beginning to realize that God knows I need the unexpected changes in my schedule.

For several years now, my life's motto has been "Blessed are the flexible for they shall never be bent out of shape." Being flexible is accepting a minor change of plans, like when our family was trying to get somewhere on time and one of our daughters—who was ready—took off her shoes and had no idea where she left them. We weren't on time.

Being flexible is accepting a major change, like when our well-scheduled week (a rare thing at our house) changed because of a phone call.

"Hello, Mom? Are you okay?"

"No, I'm watching my house burn down."

"Oh, Mom! We'll get there as quick as we can."

We abandoned the schedule and got to her as fast as we could. She moved in with us that day and stayed for a few months. After years of minor and major schedule changes, I have reached the point where I now have a sign in our house that reads, "We've had a change of schedule for Sunday, Monday, Tuesday, Wednesday, Thursday, Friday, and Saturday."

Proverbs 16:9 reminds us that, *A man's heart deviseth his way: but the LORD directeth his steps.* Arrogancy fumes about steps in a different direction than she had planned and plays the blame game. "I would have finished this if it wasn't for you." Perhaps God is teaching us to think of others before ourselves.

Arrogancy compares herself to others and, therefore, lacks wisdom.

> *For we dare not make ourselves of the number, or compare ourselves with some that commend themselves: but they measuring themselves by themselves, and comparing themselves among themselves are not wise (II Corinthians 10:12).*

Comparison is the core of Arrogancy. She is always looking around for confirmation that she is better than others. Arrogancy doesn't have the wisdom to understand that the standard is not herself but God's Word. We are all sinners in God's sight. *For all have sinned, and come short of the glory of God* (Romans 3:23). The payment for sin is the same for all. *For the wages of sin is death; but the gift of*

God is eternal life through Jesus Christ our Lord (Romans 6:23).

Eternal life is a gift not a reward. *For by grace are ye saved through faith; and that not of yourselves: it is the gift of God: Not of works, lest any man should boast* (Ephesians 2:8–9). Salvation is a gift of God and so are the abilities and responsibilities God gives by His grace.

> *Having then gifts differing according to the grace that is given to us, whether prophecy, let us prophesy according to the proportion of faith; Or ministry, let us wait on our ministering: or he that teacheth, on teaching; Or he that exhorteth, on exhortation: he that giveth, let him do it with simplicity; he that ruleth, with diligence; he that sheweth mercy, with cheerfulness* (Romans 12:6–8).

Arrogancy sees differing gifts as a way of comparing herself to others; therefore, she is not wise because she doesn't understand that God uses various gifts to make up a complete body of Christ. The eye and the little toe are both useful. It is the little things that can really make a difference. As Bob Jones, Sr. said, "The most important light in the house is not the chandelier in the parlor. It's that little back hall light that keeps you from breaking your neck when you go to the bathroom in the middle of the night."[6]

Jesus gave a great lesson on Arrogancy, which was aimed at those who were self-righteous.

> *And he spake this parable unto certain which trusted in themselves that they were righteous, and despised others: Two men went up into the temple to pray; the one a Pharisee, and the other a publican. The Pharisee stood and prayed thus with himself, God, I thank thee, that I am not as other men are, extortioners, unjust, adulterers, or even as this publican. I fast twice in the week, I give tithes of all that I possess (Luke 18:9–12).*

Notice the Pharisee compared himself to other men. He considered the standard to be his outward obedience to God's Law in certain areas. Instead of compassion, the Pharisee had contempt for the publican. That thinking leads to Arrogancy.

> *And the publican, standing afar off, would not lift up so much as his eyes unto heaven, but smote upon his breast, saying, God be merciful to me a sinner. I tell you, this man went down to his house justified rather than the other: for every one that exalteth himself shall be abased; and he that humbleth himself shall be exalted (Luke 18:13–14).*

The Pharisee went home thinking he was justified in God's sight while the publican went home actually justified in God's sight.

Beware of a self-righteous attitude. Thinking too highly of ourselves is not wise.

> *For I say, through the grace given unto me, to every man that is among you, not to think of himself more highly than he ought to think; but to think soberly, according as God hath dealt to every man the measure of faith (Romans 12:3).*

Think soberly. *Soberly*[7] is translated from the Greek word "sophroneo" (so-fron-eh'-o) meaning "to be of sound mind, sane." Do we think of ourselves with a sound mind or do we deceive ourselves? *For if a man think himself to be something, when he is nothing, he deceiveth himself* (Galatians 6:3).

Arrogancy does get silenced. In the first chapter of I Samuel, Hannah had to face Arrogancy every day from Peninnah, her husband's other wife. Peninnah had children while Hannah had none. *And her adversary also provoked her sore, for to make her fret, because the LORD had shut up her womb* (I Samuel 1:6). Notice that Peninnah is called an adversary. Like an enemy, Arrogancy stirs up guilt, shame, anger, and envy, and makes others fret. Hannah did something about this trouble—she prayed. *And she was in bitterness of soul, and prayed unto the LORD, and wept sore* (I Samuel 1:10). That was the right thing to do because the Lord knew all about Peninnah's Arrogancy and answered Hannah's prayer for a son. When Samuel was born Hannah said, *For this child I prayed; and the LORD hath given me my petition which I asked of him* (I Samuel 1:27). Hannah rejoiced in the Lord; her adversary could no longer taunt her.

> *And Hannah prayed, and said, My heart rejoiceth in the LORD, mine horn is exalted in the LORD: my mouth is enlarged over mine enemies; because I rejoice in thy salvation. There is none holy as the LORD: for there is none beside thee: neither is there any rock like our God. Talk no more so exceeding proudly; let not arrogancy come out of your mouth: for the LORD is a God of knowledge, and by him actions are weighed (I Samuel 2:1–3).*

In fact, God not only blessed Hannah with Samuel, but He also gave her three other sons and two daughters, as stated in I Samuel 2:21. Penninah couldn't taunt Hannah anymore. Arrogancy was silenced.

We hate Arrogancy in others, and we need to recognize and defeat Arrogancy in ourselves.

The Fear of the LORD Is to Hate the Evil Way

The Evil Way is against God. Stealing is the Evil Way of getting things. Fornication is the Evil Way of satisfying sexual desires. Profanity is the Evil Way of speaking. Jude 11 speaks about those who chose the Evil Way. *Woe unto them! for they have gone in the way of Cain, and ran greedily after the error of Balaam for reward, and perished in the gainsaying of Core.*

The way of Cain is the Evil Way. He was not taught the Evil Way; his parents knew the LORD and raised him in the ways of the LORD.

> *And Adam knew Eve his wife; and she conceived, and bare Cain, and said, I have gotten a man from the LORD. And she again bare his brother Abel. And Abel was a keeper of sheep, but Cain was a tiller of the ground (Genesis 4:1–2).*

The brothers experienced the same upbringing. Adam would have taught them about creation, the Garden of Eden, and how death came into the world by sin. *Wherefore, as by one man sin entered into the world, and death by sin; and so death passed upon all men, for that all have sinned* (Romans 5:12). Cain and Abel would have known that God clothed mankind. Scripture says, *Unto Adam also and to his wife did the LORD God make coats of skins, and clothed them* (Genesis 3:21). Notice that God used skins. This means God sacrificed an animal to cover Adam and Eve's nakedness. Adam would have taught his sons that God required a blood sacrifice to cover their sins. Leviticus 17:11 states, *For the life of the flesh is in the blood: and I have given it to you upon the altar to make an atonement for your souls: for it is the blood that maketh an atonement for the soul.* Even though Cain and Abel had the same home and teachings, they were not going the same way.

> *And in process of time it came to pass, that Cain brought of the fruit of the ground an offering unto the LORD. And Abel, he also brought of the firstlings of his flock and of the fat thereof. And the LORD had respect unto Abel and to his offering: But unto Cain and to his offering he had not respect. And Cain was very wroth, and his countenance fell (Genesis 4:3–5).*

The way of Cain leads to unbelief. He disregarded God's requirement for a sacrifice, blood, and brought an offering of his own choosing. He could have traded his produce for one of his brother's lambs, but he didn't. He didn't believe a lamb was the only sacrifice. Multitudes of people have followed and still follow the way of Cain. Man's religions are the result. They substitute works for Jesus, the Lamb of God. Just like Cain, religious people do that which is right in their own eyes. Rituals, religious traditions, and man's reasoning are the authority instead of God's Word. Ephesians 2:8–9 teaches, *For by grace are ye saved through faith; and that not of yourselves: it is the gift of God: Not of works, lest any man should boast.*

The way of Cain leads to murder. Cain was not willing to shed the blood of an animal, but he was willing to shed his brother's blood. Genesis 4:8 states, *And Cain talked with Abel his brother: and it came to pass, when they were in the field, that Cain rose up against Abel his brother, and slew him.* Cain was the beginning of a long line of murderers. They are described in Isaiah 59:7, which states, *Their feet run to evil, and they make haste to shed innocent blood: their thoughts are thoughts of iniquity; wasting and destruction are in their paths.* Abortion advocates follow the way of Cain; they shed innocent blood. Violent people follow the way of Cain when they destroy anyone who is righteous. It is the path of waste and destruction.

The way of Cain lacks peace. *The way of peace they know not; and there is no judgment in their goings: they have made them crooked paths: whosoever goeth therein shall not know peace* (Isaiah 59:8). A heart that is filled with hatred and thoughts of violence does not have peace. When the violent act is done, it is not peaceful to always have to look out for police. Guilt is a heavy burden, and fear of being caught makes one jumpy. *The wicked flee when no man pursueth: but the righteous are bold as a lion* (Proverbs 28:1).

The error of Balaam is the Evil Way. Balaam was a prophet. One day the princes of Moab came to him.

> *And God came unto Balaam, and said, What men are these with thee? And Balaam said unto God, Balak the son of Zippor, king of Moab, hath sent unto me, saying, Behold, there is a people come out of Egypt, which covereth the face of the earth: come now, curse me them; peradventure I shall be able to overcome them, and drive them out. And God said unto Balaam, Thou shalt not go with them;*

thou shalt not curse the people: for they are blessed (Numbers 22:9–12).

God commanded, *Thou shalt not go with them.* Balaam obeyed God and refused Balak's offer. When Balak heard of the prophet's refusal, he offered very great honour.

> *And Balak sent yet again princes, more, and more honourable than they. And they came to Balaam, and said to him, Thus saith Balak the son of Zippor, Let nothing, I pray thee, hinder thee from coming unto me: For I will promote thee unto very great honour, and I will do whatsoever thou sayest unto me: come therefore, I pray thee, curse me this people (Numbers 22:15–17).*

Balaam had already heard from God on the matter, but notice what he says to the princes. *Now therefore, I pray you, tarry ye also here this night, that I may know what the LORD will say unto me more* (Numbers 22:19). More? How can you add to "No"? Balaam wanted that reward. The Evil Way is the *error of Balaam for reward.* In this verse *error*[8] comes from the Greek word "plane" (plan'-ay), which means "a straying away." It is the sheep straying from the shepherd, *All we like sheep have gone astray; we have turned every one to his own way; and the LORD hath laid on him the iniquity of us all* (Isaiah 53:6). The love of money turns us away from faith in God. In I Timothy 6:9–10, we are warned of desiring riches.

> *But they that will be rich fall into temptation and a snare, and into many foolish and hurtful lusts, which drown men in destruction and perdition. For the love of money is the root of all evil: which while some coveted after, they have erred from the faith, and pierced themselves through with many sorrows.*

Balaam was determined to go astray for riches. He was like the sheep that keeps looking for a hole in the fence. He wouldn't rest until he found a way to get to presumably better pastures. The prophet wouldn't see the error of his way, so God sent an adversary against him—the angel of the LORD.

> *Then the LORD opened the eyes of Balaam, and he saw the angel of the LORD standing*

in the way, and his sword drawn his hand: and he bowed down his head, and fell flat on his face. And the angel of the LORD said unto him, Wherefore hast thou smitten thine ass these three times? Behold, I went out to withstand thee, because thy way is perverse before me (Numbers 22:31–32).

Notice that the angel of the LORD said, "*thy way is perverse before me.*"

Perverse[9] in Numbers 22:32 is an intransitive verb that means "to precipitate, to hurl oneself headlong." An intransitive verb is simply an action verb with no direct object. Balaam threw himself headlong on the ground before the angel of the LORD's drawn sword; he faced certain death. Notice what he says, *And Balaam said unto the angel of the LORD, I have sinned; for I knew not that thou stoodest in the way against me: now therefore, if it displease thee, I will get me back again* (Numbers 22:34). Balaam excuses his disobedience by claiming he didn't know what God wanted, yet God let him go with the princes. *And the angel of the LORD said unto Balaam, Go with the men: but only the word that I shall speak unto thee, that thou shalt speak. So Balaam went with the princes of Balak* (Numbers 22:35).

When Balaam opened his mouth, he only blessed Israel. Read Numbers 23-24 for the blessings, including prophecies of the coming Messiah. Even though Balaam spoke only blessings, he still followed the Evil Way because he was determined to please Balak in order to receive a reward. He knew how he could get God to curse the people of Israel. We learn about Balaam's evil scheme and his death in Numbers 31:8, 14–16 when God commanded Moses to go to war against the Midianites.

> *And they slew the kings of Midian, beside the rest of them that were slain; namely, Evi, and Rekem, and Zur, and Hur, and Reba, five kings of Midian: Balaam also the son of Beor they slew with the sword. [...] And Moses was wroth with the officers of the host, with the captains over thousands, and captains over hundreds, which came from the battle. And Moses said unto them, Have ye saved all the women alive? Behold, these caused the children of Israel, through the counsel of Balaam, to commit*

trespass against the LORD in the matter
of Peor, and there was a plague among the
congregation of the LORD.

The counsel of Balaam was to commit whoredom with the daughters of Moab which brought God's punishment upon Israel. Beware of following the error of Balaam. His followers are described in II Peter 2:14–15, which states:

Having eyes full of adultery, and that
cannot cease from sin; beguiling unstable
souls: an heart they have exercised with
covetous practices; cursed children: Which
have forsaken the right way, and are gone
astray, following the way of Balaam the
son of Bosor [Beor in Hebrew], who loved
the wages of unrighteousness.

We need to stay in the right way, God's way, and not follow the error of Balaam.

The gainsaying of Core is the Evil Way. *Gainsaying*[10] comes from the Greek noun *antilogia* (an-tee-log-ee'-ah) meaning "dispute, contradiction, strife." The gainsaying of Core is disputing with God-given authority. Core (Korah in Hebrew) gathered together his friends and two hundred fifty princes of Israel against Moses. Moses had not sinned, yet the mob denounced him and Aaron.

> *Now Korah, the son of Izhar, the son of Kohath, the son of Levi, and Dathan and Abiram, the sons of Eliab, and On, the son of Peleth, sons of Reuben, took men: And they rose up before Moses, with certain of the children of Israel, two hundred and fifty princes of the assembly, famous in the congregation, men of renown: And they gathered themselves together against Moses and against Aaron, and said unto them, Ye take too much upon you, seeing all the congregation are holy, every one of them, and the LORD is among them: wherefore then lift ye up yourselves above the congregation of the LORD? (Numbers 16:1–3).*

Pride and Arrogancy were at work. Core and his followers compared themselves to Moses and Aaron. They accused them of being in command by their own choosing, saying, "*wherefore then lift ye up yourselves above the congregation of the LORD?*"

That was a lie. God had chosen Moses. *Come now therefore, and I will send thee unto Pharaoh, that thou mayest bring forth my people the children of Israel out of Egypt* (Exodus 3:10). Since Moses protested that he was slow of speech, God chose Aaron to be Moses' spokesman to the people.

> *And the anger of the LORD was kindled against Moses, and he said, Is not Aaron the Levite thy brother? I know that he can speak well. And also, behold, he cometh forth to meet thee: and when he seeth thee, he will be glad in his heart (Exodus 4:14).*

The gainsaying of Core is the battle of words which consists of false accusations and lies. There is no reason for the dispute. Do we dispute with our God-chosen authority simply because we don't want to accept that authority? There is no sin on the part of the authority. The heart of the problem is rebellion against the Lord. Core and the princes wanted the leadership position God had given Moses and Aaron.

> *And Moses said unto Korah, Hear, I pray you, ye sons of Levi: Seemeth it but a small*

thing unto you, that the God of Israel hath separated you from the congregation of Israel, to bring you near to himself to do the service of the tabernacle of the LORD, and to stand before the congregation to minister unto them? And he hath brought thee near to him, and all thy brethren the sons of Levi with thee: and seek ye the priesthood also? For which cause both thou and all thy company are gathered together against the LORD: and what is Aaron, that ye murmur against him (Numbers 16:8–11)?

We have been given authorities in our lives. Be careful not to follow someone who stirs up strife against authority. Whether we like God-given authority or not, our response to that authority should be to obey and pray.

Do we teach children to obey and pray for their parents? Scripture says, *Children, obey your parents in all things: for this is well pleasing unto the Lord* (Colossians 3:20). Respect for authority begins with respect for parents.

Are we obeying and praying for our husbands? A wife is a powerful witness when she submits to her husband's authority and prays for him. There are wives who have led their unsaved husbands to the Lord, and it started with obedience. *Likewise, ye wives, be in subjection to your own husbands; that, if any obey not the word, they also may without the word be won by the conversation of the wives; While they behold your chaste conversation coupled with fear* (I Peter 3:1–2). Sarah is our example of obedience. *Even as Sara obeyed Abraham, calling him lord: whose daughters ye are, as long as ye do well, and are not afraid with any amazement* (I Peter 3:6). I call my husband Anthony "me lord," and I am his lady. Chivalry lives!

Do we obey and pray for our pastors? *Obey them that have the rule over you, and submit yourselves: for they watch for your souls, as they that must give account, that they may do it with joy, and not with grief: for that is unprofitable for you* (Hebrews 13:17). October is Pastor Appreciation Month, and the best way to show appreciation is to follow the pastor's leadership. Write him a "thank you" note, especially for a message that blessed you or something he did for you. Pray for him and his family daily to have wisdom and strength.

Do we obey and pray for our employers? *Servants, obey in all things your masters according to the flesh; not with eyeservice, as menpleasers; but in singleness of heart, fearing God: And whatsoever ye do, do it heartily, as to the Lord, and not unto men* (Colossians 3:22–23). Doing things to please the Lord puts a positive perspective on any job.

Do we obey and pray for our government officials? *I exhort therefore, that, first of all, supplications, prayers, intercessions, and giving of thanks, be made for all men; For kings, and for all that are in authority; that we may lead a quiet and peaceable life in all godliness and honesty* (I Timothy 2:1–2). Instead of complaining about the government, we should be asking God to provide wisdom to our local and national leaders. Pray for their salvation.

Since Moses had his God-given authority challenged before the congregation, he refuted the lie before the whole congregation. *And Moses said, Hereby ye shall know that the LORD hath sent me to do all these works; for I have not done them of mine own mind* (Numbers 16:28). He then substantiated his authority by declaring that those who provoked the LORD would die.

> *If these men die the common death of all men, or if they be visited after the visitation of all men; then the LORD hath not sent me. But if the LORD make a new thing, and the earth open her mouth, and swallow them up, with all that appertain unto them, and they go down quick into the pit; then ye shall understand that these men have provoked the LORD (Numbers 16:29–30).*

Moses certainly did not have the power to open the ground. Those words came from the LORD, and it happened just as Moses said.

> *And it came to pass, as he had made an end of speaking all these words, that the ground clave asunder that was under them: And the earth opened her mouth, and swallowed them up, and their houses, and all the men that appertained unto Korah, and all their goods. They, and all*

that appertained to them, went down alive into the pit, and the earth closed upon them: and they perished from among the congregation (Numbers 16:31–33).

The battle of words was over. We hate the Evil Way of others and must recognize and defeat any Evil Way in ourselves.

The Fear of the LORD Is to Hate the Froward Mouth

The Froward Mouth is evil. Scripture states, *A naughty person, a wicked man, walketh with a froward mouth* (Proverbs 6:12). Swear words, euphemisms for God, slander, and perverse speech come from a Froward Mouth. Members of a criminal gang aren't the only ones guilty of a Froward Mouth. The Pharisees, those that were self-righteous, were guilty of speaking evil. Jesus said to them, *O generation of vipers, how can ye, being evil, speak good things? for out of the abundance of the heart the mouth speaketh* (Matthew 12:34).

What is in your heart, your thoughts and your feelings, will eventually come out of your mouth. The

Pharisees revealed their thoughts about John the Baptist and Jesus with their Froward Mouth. Jesus told the multitude,

> For John came neither eating nor drinking, and they say, He hath a devil. The Son of man came eating and drinking, and they say, Behold a man gluttonous, and a winebibber, a friend of publicans and sinners. But wisdom is justified of her children (Matthew 11:18–19).

The envy and disbelief in the Pharisees' hearts came out of their Froward Mouths as lies. Jesus never violated His Word, as it says, *Be not among winebibbers; among riotous eaters of flesh: For the drunkard and the glutton shall come to poverty: and drowsiness shall clothe a man with rags* (Proverbs 23:20–21). The Froward Mouth uses slander to defame those with a good name. It has destroyed careers, marriages, friendships, and ministries.

The Froward Mouth is an unruly evil. This is the reason people will excuse their words by saying, "I can't help it. I just say what I think," as if it's necessary to let others know their thoughts.

For every kind of beasts, and of birds, and of serpents, and of things in the sea, is tamed, and hath been tamed of mankind: But the tongue can no man tame; it is an unruly evil, full of deadly poison. Therewith bless we God, even the Father; and therewith curse we men, which are made after the similitude of God. Out of the same mouth proceedeth blessing and cursing. My brethren, these things ought not so to be (James 3:7–10).

Words reveal much about a person. *For the wicked boasteth of his heart's desire, and blesseth the covetous, whom the LORD abhorreth. [...] His mouth is full of cursing and deceit and fraud: under his tongue is mischief and vanity* (Psalm 10:3,7). Consider the words of the wicked as follows:

The Froward Mouth boasts about his heart's desire.

Go to now, ye that say, Today or tomorrow we will go into such a city, and continue there a year, and buy and sell, and get gain: Whereas ye know not what shall be on the morrow. For what is your life? It is even a vapour, that appeareth for a little time, and then vanisheth away. For that ye ought to say, if the Lord will, we shall live, and do this, or that. But now ye rejoice in your boastings: all such rejoicing is evil (James 4:13–16).

Why is boasting about our future plans evil, you ask? Because it comes from a heart of Pride. Boasting says:

"I will…"

"I am going to…"

"I can…"

Lord willing, we will do what we planned. Unexpected company may arrive. The car won't start. Someone calls in need of immediate help. The good health we enjoyed is suddenly gone. When my dad was battling cancer, he would say, "Every day is a gift from God." How true! The important time is now.

Besides boasting, the Froward Mouth blesses those who covet.

"Where did you get that?"

"It was in someone's yard. I've always wanted one of these."

"Did they see you take it?"

"No, no one was home."

"Good thing. They can always get another one."

That is an example of blessing those who covet. It encourages others to envy what is not theirs or commend them for stealing and not getting caught. Shoplifters have this mentality. Their thinking is "The store can afford to lose this item." It is evil. God commands *Thou shalt not covet thy neighbour's house, thou shalt not covet thy neighbour's wife, nor his manservant, nor his maidservant, nor his ox, nor his ass, nor any thing that is thy neighbour's* (Exodus 20:17).

The Froward Mouth is full of cursing. Cursing is the opposite of blessing. They are words spoken to invoke evil, to speak damnation, or to crave destruction. It's saying to someone, "Drop dead." Obviously, these words are often spoken in anger and bitterness. Jesus taught in His Sermon on the Mount:

> *Ye have heard that it hath been said, Thou shalt love thy neighbour, and hate thine enemy. But I say unto you, Love your enemies, bless them that curse you, do good to them that hate you, and pray for them which despitefully use you, and persecute you: That ye may be the children of your Father which is in heaven: for he maketh his sun to rise on the evil and on the good, and sendeth rain on the just and on the unjust (Matthew 5:43–45).*

Jesus is teaching how to respond to the one who curses you—bless them instead. When someone says, "Razz ma tazz" to you, respond kindly with, "God bless you." Saying "God bless you" is a ray of sunshine on a dark day. Do evil people thank God for the sunshine? No, but He lets it shine on them anyway. Ecclesiastes has another thought for us. *Also take no heed unto all words that are spoken; lest thou hear thy servant curse thee: For oftentimes also thine own heart knoweth that thou thyself likewise hast cursed others* (Ecclesiastes 7:21–22). It's our fleshly nature to get angry with those who curse us, yet we excuse ourselves for cursing others. Has anyone not yelled at another driver?

A man was in a friend's car and noticed a piece of paper taped to the dashboard that read "FIDO."

"Is that your dog's name?"

"No."

"What is it?"

"It's a reminder to myself not to get angry at a dumb driver. It stands for, 'Forget It and Drive On.'" (This is a true story.)

The Froward Mouth speaks deceit and fraud.

Deceit and fraud are the hallmarks of a liar. Such a person cannot be trusted to tell the truth. Aesop's fable, *The Boy Who Cried Wolf*, is a perfect example. A shepherd boy kept interrupting harvesters in a nearby field by crying out, "Wolf, wolf!" But there was no wolf. After a few times of running to the rescue and finding no wolf, the harvesters ignored the boy's cries when a wolf really did appear and attack the flock. Even when a liar tells the truth, he will have already lost all credibility, and no one will believe him. If we make up lies, leave out facts, or completely change the story, we are guilty of deceit and fraud.

Not long ago we were looking for a particular wheelchair van for my handicapped brother who lives with us. Online we found a dealership in Michigan that had a large inventory. The website showed a wheelchair van that appeared to be the answer to our prayers. I talked to a salesman and the manager to get all the information about the van, and I was willing to make the more than ten-hour round-trip drive. Our daughter and grandchildren drove us since we were planning to drive the wheelchair van back home. Upon arrival, we saw that the van was a 2016 model, not the 2017 as it was advertised online. I spoke with the manager about it.

"Excuse me," I said, "but on your website this van is listed as a 2017."

"Oh, no, it's a 2016. It must have been listed wrong," the manager replied.

"The mileage is not the same either," I said. "This van was listed as having just over eleven thousand miles. It shows here that it has over thirty-four thousand miles."

"Oh, no, this van never had eleven thousand miles because when it came here it already had twenty-nine thousand miles."

We went inside the van and noticed the space between the back seats. I questioned the manager again.

"Are you sure a wheelchair twenty-seven inches wide will fit between these seats? The space looks rather narrow. I gave you the dimensions of the wheelchair over the phone."

"Oh, no. There's no way a wheelchair will fit between these seats. It's only twenty-four inches."

We decided not to do business with that dealership due to the obvious deceit. As an American consumer would say, "He who lies to customer loses business."

The Froward Mouth speaks mischief and vanity. *Be not thou envious against evil men, neither desire to be with them. For their heart studieth destruction, and their lips talk of mischief* (Proverbs 24:1–2). Mischief is not a blessing; it is intentional hurt, embarrassment, or trouble for someone. How our flesh wants to do mischief! I can seem clever if I tell others how clumsy and foolish they are. Vanity comes into play here. It's looking in the mirror and saying, "Mirror, mirror, on the wall, who is the cleverest of them all?" As God's ambassador in this sinful world, I am to represent my Lord Jesus in my speech. *Put away from thee a froward mouth, and perverse lips put far from thee* (Proverbs 4:24).

We hate the Froward Mouth of others, and we must recognize and defeat our Froward Mouth.

Further Study for Fear of the LORD

Look up the following verses and answer the questions.

1. Read Deuteronomy 6:24; 10:12–13. Why are we to Fear the LORD?

2. Read Job 28:28. According to this verse, what is wisdom?

3. Read Psalm 19:9. What two truths are given about Fear of the LORD?

4. Read Psalm 36:11. How is Pride described in this verse?

5. Read I Corinthians 1:11–13. How was Arrogancy evident in the church at Corinth?

6. Read III John 9–11. How was Diotrephes following the Evil Way in the church?

7. Read Proverbs 10:31. The expression *"be cut out"* in this verse has the same meaning as the Hebrew expression *"cut off"* used in Psalm 12:3, Psalm 34:16,

and Micah 5:8–13. What does this expression say will happen to the Froward Mouth?

8. Read Psalm 115:12–13. Who will the LORD bless?

Pillar #2

Instruction

————— ✝ —————

The fear of the LORD is the instruction of wisdom; and before honour is humility (Proverbs 15:33).

Hear instruction, and be wise, and refuse it not (Proverbs 8:33). If we are to be wise, we must listen and learn. A wise man will hear, and will increase learning; and a man of understanding shall attain unto wise counsels (Proverbs 1:5). To hear Instruction we must pay attention to the one speaking.

I remember a particular Sunday morning at Calvary Baptist Church in Iowa when the congregation was shaking hands. A brother in Christ shook my hand, and I cheerfully asked, "Hi, how are you?"

"Not good at all," he replied.

"That's good," I said. I turned to greet someone else before realizing what the man had said to me. I was not really listening. We can do the same thing during a Sunday school class or a sermon. Are we actually listening to Instruction or letting our minds wander?

For example, the church service begins and we start looking around us. "I see Mildred has a new dress. That's the perfect color for her. I should go clothes shopping this week. Excuse me, what verse did Pastor say? I really should take time to memorize the books of the minor prophets. Micah is a nice name."

Hearing Instruction begins when we are children. *Hear, ye children, the instruction of a father, and attend to know understanding* (Proverbs 4:1). Think of the things we have had to learn. We had to be taught how to talk, to be polite, and to obey authority. *Children, obey your parents in the Lord:*

for this is right (Ephesians 6:1). Learning is the foundation for the rest of our lives. For example, my father and mother taught us children to be home at the set time from playing at the neighbors' house. If we were going to be late, we should call. They were teaching us accountability.

Receiving Instruction

Our heavenly Father tells us to receive Instruction because it has great value. *Receive my instruction, and not silver; and knowledge rather than choice gold* (Proverbs 8:10). *Receive*[11] in that verse translates from *laqach* (law-kakh'), in Hebrew, which means "to take in, to accept." Just as we breathe in oxygen, we should hear Instruction. By accepting Instruction, we will do what we have learned from God's Word, and stay on the right path. *He is in the way of life that keepeth instruction* (Proverbs 10:17a).

Adam's son, Abel, obeyed his father's Instruction about the necessity of bringing a blood sacrifice, and God accepted Abel's lamb. It will be evident that we have listened to God's Instruction when we choose to be obedient and gain wisdom. As Proverbs 9:9 says, *Give instruction to a wise man, and he will be yet wiser: teach a just man, and he will increase in learning.*

In *The Wise Pupil,* by Mabel Watts, the teacher instructed seven young men in reading, writing, and arithmetic. At the same time, he taught them courage, honesty, and patience. When they were old enough to earn their own living, the teacher gave them a strange final exam. Each student was issued a gold coin and told to fill an empty room with something he judged worthwhile. That way the teacher would see if the students had learned the lessons he had taught.

The first student showed up the next day to display a room full of chopped wood for burning. He thought keeping warm and comfortable was worthwhile. The teacher was not impressed. The second student bought a plump hen. He intended to sell eggs at a good price. When the hen was too old to lay, he would invite relatives over for a feast and would make a down comforter with the feathers. The teacher told him that he could have done better. The third pupil bought a cow, so he could have milk to drink and make butter and cheese to sell. [He must have been the son of a Wisconsin farmer.]

Again, the teacher told the student he could have done better. The fourth student bought a horse to ride far and wide. He would write about his travels and become rich from his writing. The teacher admired the horse and moved to the next room. The fifth student filled it with food. The teacher said that was sensible then looked into the sixth room. It was empty. That student hadn't been able to make up his mind and bought nothing. The teacher shook his head. The seventh student opened the door to reveal a small oil lamp and extra oil. After a day's work, he would light the lamp and continue his studies. Perhaps, one day, he could teach others what he learned. The teacher was pleased.

We must continuously study Instruction in God's Word. We will never be able to say, "I have learned it all." We can also teach others what we have learned.

God commands us to take fast hold of Instruction. *Take fast hold of instruction; let her not go: keep her; for she is thy life* (Proverbs 4:13). Think of Instruction as a life preserver. If someone falls over-board, he can grab onto a life preserver to keep from drowning. The life preserver is the means of survival. God's Instruction keeps us from drowning in the depths of doubt, despair, and darkness of sin. It keeps us living for God amidst the waves and strong currents of man's ideas and philosophies. God warns us, *Beware lest any man spoil you through philosophy and vain deceit, after the tradition of men, after the rudiments of the world, and not after Christ* (Colossians 2:8).

The word *spoil*[12] in that verse comes from the Greek word *sylagogeo* (soo-lag-ogue-eh'-o), which means "to lead away from the truth and subject to one's sway." Feminist ideas try to pull us away from God's role of a wife and mother. For example, a feminist would tell us it's fine to work at a day care to watch another woman's child, but you're oppressed if you are at home caring for your own children. Titus 2:3–5 states:

> *The aged women likewise, that they be in behaviour as becometh holiness, not false accusers, not given to much wine, teachers of good things; That they may teach the young women to be sober, to love their husbands, to love their children, To be discreet, chaste, keepers at home, good, obedient to*

*their own husbands, that the word of God
be not blasphemed.*

Notice God provides specific Instruction to wives
and mothers in that passage *that the word of God
be not blasphemed.* The word *blasphemed*[13] comes
from the Greek word *blasphemeo* (blas-fay-meh'-o),
which means "to vilify, to speak evil, defame, revile."
When we obey Instruction, we show the truth of
the Word of God, and it will not be blasphemed.

We can also receive Instruction by observing.
Solomon was riding in his chariot one day when he
saw a field and a vineyard that caught his attention.

> *I went by the field of the slothful, and by
> the vineyard of the man void of under-
> standing; And, lo, it was all grown over
> with thorns, and nettles had covered the
> face thereof, and the stone wall thereof
> was broken down. Then I saw, and con-
> sidered it well: I looked upon it, and
> received instruction. Yet a little sleep, a
> little slumber, a little folding of the hands
> to sleep: So shall thy poverty come as one*

*that travelleth; and thy want as an armed
man (Proverbs 24:30–34).*

By observing the field of the slothful, Solomon
wrote that he received Instruction— the lazy end
up in poverty and suffer from want. *Aesop's Fables*
has a story entitled *The Grasshopper and the Ant*.
The grasshopper played all summer while the ant
worked hard to gather food for winter. When winter
came, the ant was well fed and warm, but the grasshopper was starving and cold. The lesson is that we
are to be like the ant. Proverbs 6:6-8 also supports
this thought. *Go to the ant, thou sluggard; consider
her ways, and be wise: Which having no guide, overseer, or ruler, Provideth her meat in the summer, and
gathereth her food in the harvest.* The Instruction is
to observe ants and work like them.

II Thessalonians 3:10–11 states:

> *For even when we were with you, this we
> commanded you, that if any would not
> work, neither should he eat. For we hear
> that there are some which walk among
> you disorderly, working not at all, but are
> busybodies.*

Learn to be busy working like an ant instead of being idle.

Observing consequences gives us Instruction. We don't have to try something to see if it will hurt us or not. For example, seeing what drinking alcohol has done to various relatives, I have learned that alcohol is evil. It ruins marriages and families. It causes car accidents and leaves car occupants crippled or dead. It kills brain cells, damages the liver, and wrecks overall health. *Wine is a mocker, strong drink is raging: and whosoever is deceived thereby is not wise* (Proverbs 20:1). Other addictive substances also have terrible effects. The good news is I have seen what Jesus can do in a life that is obedient to His Word. There truly is victory in Jesus.

Instruction in righteousness is the key to a godly life, and Instruction comes from Scripture. *All scripture is given by inspiration of God, and is profitable for doctrine, for reproof, for correction, for instruction in righteousness: That the man of God may be perfect, throughly furnished unto all good works* (II Timothy 3:16–17). Instruction in righteousness teaches us to:

- Speak truth: *He that speaketh truth sheweth forth righteousness* (Proverbs 12:17a).

- Sin not: *Awake to righteousness, and sin not; for some have not the knowledge of God: I speak this to your shame* (I Corinthians 15:34).

- Separate from unbelievers: *Be ye not unequally yoked together with unbelievers: for what fellowship hath righteousness with unrighteousness? and what communion hath light with darkness* (II Corinthians 6:14)?

Let me clarify the teaching here. The purpose of a yoke is to keep two animals joined together to pull a wagon, plow, or cart. It would be two oxen, two horses, or two cattle. No farmer would think of joining a sheep and an ox in a yoke. The goal would be to get somewhere, haul a load, or accomplish something. As a sheep of God's pasture, I would be unequally yoked with people who are not sheep. Consider the goals and messages endorsed by clubs, organizations, and teams, as well as that attractive man with a warm smile. Would we be equally yoked or unequally yoked with them?

When Hazel Benton got saved, she told her pastor that she would not be attending the Sunday evening services because she was in a bowling league. When she heard the Instruction that she should be with other believers in church, she quit the bowling league. Hazel became a faithful church member and a bold witness for Christ. I had the opportunity to be her soulwinning partner many times. It was always inspiring to see Hazel hand out tracts on the streets of Chicago and talk to strangers about receiving Jesus as their Saviour. She never regretted quitting the bowling league.

By being separate from unbelievers, does that mean we cannot go to an unbeliever's house? No. Jesus accepted invitations to eat with unbelievers. We have plenty of unsaved relatives, and we do visit and eat with them, but we are new creatures in Christ. II Corinthians 5:17 says, *Therefore if any man be in Christ, he is a new creature: old things are passed away; behold, all things are become new.* For example, when I was a child, my family never prayed before meals. After being saved and receiving Instruction about giving thanks to the Lord, I started praying before meals. It still serves as a way to witness to unbelieving relatives.

Refusing Instruction

God warns us that refusing Instruction will bring poverty and shame. *Poverty and shame shall be to him that refuseth instruction: but he that regardeth reproof shall be honoured* (Proverbs 13:18). For instance, Scripture has Instruction on receiving wealth. Remember the ant? God instructs us to work diligently. We also learn what happens to an idle employee who refuses Instruction and does not work hard. *He becometh poor that dealeth with a slack hand: but the hand of the diligent maketh rich* (Proverbs 10:4). An idle employee will eventually quit or be fired and then complain about not having money.

Refusing Instruction about giving to the LORD also leads to poverty. In the days of Haggai, people were indifferent about rebuilding the Lord's house. God withheld his blessings.

> *Thus speaketh the LORD of hosts, saying, This people say, The time is not come, the time that the LORD's house should be built. Then came the word of the LORD by Haggai the prophet, saying, Is it time*

for you, O ye, to dwell in your cieled houses, and this house lie waste? Now therefore thus saith the LORD of hosts; Consider your ways. Ye have sown much, and bring in little; ye eat, but ye have not enough; ye drink, but ye are not filled with drink; ye clothe you, but there is none warm; and he that earneth wages earneth wages to put it into a bag with holes (Haggai 1:2-6).

Sounds like God would not let His people enjoy prosperity with what should have be given to God.

Refusing Instruction can lead to death. Jungle explorers who carried adequate clothing and equipment have died of starvation. Their food supply ran out, and they did not take the time to listen to natives about jungle plants that provided fresh water and would be safe to eat. In the same way, men and women who have adequate morals, pay their bills on time, obey the laws of the land, attend church regularly, and are good neighbors, have died of soul starvation. They didn't have the Bread of Life—Jesus.

And Jesus said unto them, I am the bread of life: he that cometh to me shall never hunger; and he that believeth on me shall never thirst. [...] Verily, verily, I say unto you, He that believeth on me hath everlasting life. I am that bread of life (John 6:35, 47–48).

Have you received Jesus or is your soul starving to death? *He that refuseth instruction despiseth his own soul* (Proverbs 15:32a).

Further Study for Instruction

Look up the verses then answer the questions.

1. Read II Kings 12:1–2.
    a. Who was the instructor?
    b. Who was taught?
    c. What was the Instruction?

2. Read I Chronicles 25:5–7.
    a. Who were the three instructors?
    b. What was the Instruction?
    c. What was the total number of those instructed?

3. Read II Timothy 1:1–2, 4–5; 3:15.
    a. Who were the instructors?
    b. Who was taught?
    c. What was the Instruction?

4. Read Jeremiah 28:15–17.
    a. Who had been the instructor?
    b. Who had been taught?
    c. What had been taught?
    d. What happened to the instructor?

5. Read Mark 9:31–32.
    a. Who was the instructor?
    b. Who was being taught?
    c. What were they taught?
    d. Why didn't they ask for an explanation?

Knowledge

———— ✝ ————

The fear of the LORD is the beginning of knowledge: but fools despise wisdom and instruction (Proverbs 1:7).

Knowledge of God

Yea, if thou criest after knowledge, and liftest up thy voice for understanding; If thou seekest her as silver, and searchest for her as for hid treasures; Then shalt thou understand the fear of the LORD, and find the knowledge of God* (Proverbs 2:3–5). Who is God? Our view of God will determine our response to Him. If we see God as indifferent or mean, we will probably not seek Him. We can gain Knowledge of God by studying His names. This would be a whole study in itself, so we'll look at the two most important names. *Elohim*[14] (el-lo-heem') is the Hebrew name which is commonly translated "God" in English. It is the plural form which means "the Supreme God, the Mighty." This name is used for God in Genesis 1:1, which states, *In the beginning God created the heaven and the earth.* The power of His Word created light. *And God said, Let there be light: and there was light* (Genesis 1:3). God's power created nitrogen, oxygen, argon, carbon dioxide, and other gases. *Elohim* also combined two explosive elements—hydrogen and oxygen—and made water. *And God said, Let there be a firmament in the midst of the waters, and let it divide the waters from the waters* (Genesis 1:6). He created dry land and caused plants to spring up from the ground. Ever study a green leaf? It is a manufacturing plant (pun intended) in itself. *And God said, Let the earth bring forth grass, the herb yielding seed, and the fruit tree yielding fruit after his kind, whose seed is in itself, upon the earth: and it was so* (Genesis 1:11). God's power hung the sun, moon, and stars in place.

> *And God said, Let there be lights in the firmament of the heaven to divide the day from the night; and let them be for signs, and for seasons, and for days, and years:*

And let them be for lights in the firmament
of the heaven to give light upon the earth:
and it was so (Genesis 1:14–15).

He numbered and named the stars. *He telleth the*
number of the stars; he calleth them all by their
names (Psalm 147:4). The power of His Word pro-
duced salmon, jellyfish, sharks, clams, and whales,
as well as fowl to fly in the air. *Elohim* designed the
oyster that produces pearls and the hummingbird
that can fly any direction and hover. *And God said,*
Let the waters bring forth abundantly the moving
creature that hath life, and fowl that may fly above
the earth in the open firmament of heaven (Genesis
1:20). God created land animals. *And God said, Let*
the earth bring forth the living creature after his kind,
cattle, and creeping thing, and beast of the earth after
his kind: and it was so (Genesis 1:24). Dinosaurs are
included in beasts of the earth. Think about it. God
created all animals. Dinosaurs are animals; therefore, God created dinosaurs. He knew what He was
doing. Ever notice that the biggest land animals are
herbivores, plant eaters? God is the wise Creator.

Elohim is also used in the short form, *El,* which
means "might, power." This is seen in the name

El-Shaddai[15] (el shad-di'), which translates to "Almighty God." The patriarchs were the first to hear God's name as *El-Shaddai*. *And when Abram was ninety years old and nine, the LORD appeared to Abram, and said unto him, I am the Almighty God; walk before me, and be thou perfect* (Genesis 17:1). Isaac used that name for God when blessing Jacob.

> *Arise, go to Padan-aram, to the house of Bethuel thy mother's father; and take thee a wife from thence of the daughters of Laban thy mother's brother. And God Almighty bless thee, and make thee fruitful, and multiply thee, that thou mayest be a multitude of people (Genesis 28:2–3).*

Years later, when Jacob returned with his wives and children, God told Jacob that He was *El-Shaddai*.

> *And God said unto him, Thy name is Jacob: thy name shall not be called any more Jacob, but Israel shall be thy name: and he called his name Israel. And God said unto him, I am God Almighty: be fruitful and multiply; a nation and a company of nations shall be of thee, and kings shall*

come out of thy loins; And the land which I gave Abraham and Isaac, to thee I will give it, and to thy seed after thee will I give the land (Genesis 35:10–11).

It is no wonder that the nation of Israel exists today. *El-Shaddai* gave the land to the descendants of Jacob—the Jews.

The other chief name for God is *Jehovah*[16] (je-hoe'vah), translated "LORD," meaning "the self-Existent or Eternal." Man was created by the hands of *Jehovah* unlike the rest of creation which had come into existence by *Elohim* speaking. *And the LORD God formed man of the dust of the ground, and breathed into his nostrils the breath of life; and man became a living soul* (Genesis 2:7). He is the Potter, and we are the clay. *But now, O LORD, thou art our father; we are the clay, and thou our potter; and we all are the work of thy hand* (Isaiah 64:8). With His hands, *Jehovah* made a woman.

And the LORD God caused a deep sleep to fall upon Adam, and he slept: and he took one of his ribs, and closed up the flesh instead thereof; And the rib, which the

*LORD God had taken from man, made he
a woman, and brought her unto the man
(Genesis 2:21–22).*

We may be awed by sculptures such as *The Thinker*
created by Auguste Rodin but look what God made!
He designed and formed the skeletal system, the
respiratory system, and the circulatory system. Our
network of nerves is fantastic. God formed eyes,
skin, hair, and even toes. If we stopped to consider the complexity of the brain, we would have
to acknowledge God as the Creator. As it says in
Psalm139:14, *I will praise thee; for I am fearfully
and wonderfully made: marvellous are thy works;
and that my soul knoweth right well.*

Jehovah or "LORD" is also another name for
Jesus Christ.

*Behold, the days come, saith the LORD,
that I will raise unto David a righteous
Branch, and a King shall reign and prosper,
and shall execute judgment and justice in
the earth. In his days Judah shall be saved,
and Israel shall dwell safely: and this is his*

name whereby he shall be called, the LORD
our righteousness (Jeremiah 23:5–6).

Old Testament prophets looked for the coming of the Messiah, or the coming of *Jehovah*. Zechariah said, *Sing and rejoice, O daughter of Zion: for, lo, I come, and I will dwell in the midst of thee, saith the LORD* (Zechariah 2:10). Jesus is the LORD God.

> *In the beginning was the Word, and the Word was with God, and the Word was God. The same was in the beginning with God. […] And the Word was made flesh, and dwelt among us, (and we beheld his glory, the glory as of the only begotten of the Father,) full of grace and truth (John 1:1–2, 14).*

The hands that formed man from the dust of the ground became the child's hands that grasped the hands of Mary and Joseph. As Jesus grew into a man, He held a hammer and built things. Later, His hands brought healing to the sick, the blind, and the deaf. He cleansed the lepers and raised the dead. *The LORD openeth the eyes of the blind: the LORD raiseth them that are bowed down: the LORD loveth the righteous* (Psalm 146:8). He broke bread with His hands to feed a multitude. One day, Jesus' hands were nailed to a cross to pay the penalty of our sins.

> *My strength is dried up like a potsherd; and my tongue cleaveth to my jaws; and thou hast brought me into the dust of death. For dogs have compassed me: the assembly of the wicked have inclosed me: they pierced my hands and my feet (Psalm 22:15–16).*

After three days and nights, Jesus' hands folded the napkin that had covered His face. He had risen!

At the tomb, the angel spoke to Mary Magdalene and the other Mary, saying, *And the angel answered and said unto the women, Fear not ye: for I know that ye seek Jesus, which was crucified. He is not here: for he is risen, as he said. Come, see the place where the Lord lay* (Matthew 28:5–6).

Praise the Lord! The Knowledge of God allows us to praise and worship Him.

> *The LORD is gracious, and full of compassion; slow to anger, and of great mercy. The*

LORD is good to all: and his tender mercies are over all his works. All thy works shall praise thee, O LORD; and thy saints shall bless thee (Psalm 145:8–10).

As the hymn writer Carl Boberg proclaimed, "How Great Thou Art!"

Knowledge of Man

As we already know, man is a created being. *So God created man in his own image, in the image of God created he him; male and female created he them* (Genesis 1:27). God called the first man Adam[17] which means "ruddy" or red. It refers to the dust of the ground that God used to form man.

Man was created with intellect. Adam's first recorded act in the Garden of Eden was to name the beasts and the fowls.

And out of the ground the LORD God formed every beast of the field, and every fowl of the air; and brought them unto Adam to see what he would call them: and whatsoever Adam called every living creature, that was the name thereof (Genesis 2:19).

Parents have trouble naming one child and that's with the help of a long list baby names. Adam named the animals without the help of anything or anyone. He was very smart. Man's reasoning power was shown when God made Adam a wife. He understood that the woman came from his side; therefore, they were one flesh. *And Adam said, This is now bone of my bones, and flesh of my flesh: she shall be called Woman, because she was taken out of Man* (Genesis 2:23). After the Fall of man, Adam gave his wife a name. No children had been born to them yet, but Adam believed God's promise of a Saviour and that the woman would bring forth children. *And Adam called his wife's name Eve; because she was the mother of all living* (Genesis 3:20). Eve[18] in Hebrew is *Chavvah* (khav-vaw') meaning "life-giver." Adam could think and reason.

Man was created to work. Even in a perfect environment, Adam was not to sit, eat, and fall asleep. *And the LORD God took the man, and put him into the garden of Eden to dress it and to keep it* (Genesis 2:15). The action verb *dress*[19] comes from the Hebrew word *abad* (aw-bad') which means "to work." Adam worked in the Garden of Eden. The same word *abad* is translated "till" in Genesis 3:23, which states, *Therefore the LORD God sent him forth from the garden of Eden, to till the ground from whence he was taken.*

Adam was a gardener before and after the Fall of man, but after the Fall the ground was cursed. He would have to work hard and sweat. Any of us who have weeded a large garden, or picked row after row of green beans, or worked in the hayfields on a hot summer day know about hard work and sweat.

> *And unto Adam he said, Because thou hast hearkened unto the voice of thy wife, and hast eaten of the tree, of which I commanded thee, saying, Thou shalt not eat of it: cursed is the ground for thy sake; in sorrow shalt thou eat of it all the days of thy life; Thorns also and thistles shall it bring forth to thee; and thou shalt eat the herb of the field; In the sweat of thy face shalt thou eat bread, till thou return unto the ground; for out of it wast thou taken:*

for dust thou art, and unto dust shalt thou return (Genesis 3:17–19).

Adam's work in the Garden of Eden was also to keep it. *And the LORD God took the man, and put him into the garden of Eden to dress it and to keep it* (Genesis 2:15). The word *keep*[20] is from the Hebrew word *shamar* (shaw-mar'), which means "to guard, to protect." It's the same word used in Genesis 3:24, which states, *So he [the LORD God] drove out the man; and he placed at the east of the garden of Eden Cherubims, and a flaming sword which turned every way, to keep the way of the tree of life.* Adam was supposed to protect the garden and should have driven out the enemy, the serpent. Instead, God drove Adam and Eve out of the garden.

A primary Sunday school teacher taught about Adam and Eve in the Garden of Eden and the Fall of man. Afterward, the teacher asked students to draw a picture of what they learned. She noticed that one boy drew a car with people in it.

"What is this?" the teacher asked.

"It's God driving Adam and Eve out of the garden," he said.

Man was created with a will. He could make decisions. God gave Adam a command and then God let Adam decide if he would obey or not obey. *And the LORD God commanded the man, saying, Of every tree of the garden thou mayest freely eat: But of the tree of the knowledge of good and evil, thou shalt not eat of it: for in the day that thou eatest thereof thou shalt surely die* (Genesis 2:16–17).

Adam had the Knowledge God wanted him to have; His Word was the Knowledge. The first man knew what God had commanded and why. Adam chose to eat of the tree, in direct violation of God's command, and brought death into the world.

> *Wherefore, as by one man sin entered into the world, and death by sin; and so death passed upon all men, for that all have sinned:[...] Nevertheless death reigned from Adam to Moses, even over them that had not sinned after the similitude of Adam's transgression, who is the figure of him that was to come (Romans 5:12,14).*

We sometimes struggle to accept that God gave man a will of his own. God wanted fellowship with man; a fellowship based on love not forced obedience. We can understand that. A father asks two of his children to go with him to bring flowers to the local assisted living center. One sits in the car grumbling while the other talks with his father and has a good time. Both children are in the car, but only one is having fellowship with the father. The child talking with the father wants to be with him and bring flowers to the elderly residents. The father would like both children to enjoy being with him and doing things together. That's what God desires. He wants His children to enjoy His presence and help in His work because they want a close relationship with Him. God lets man decide instead of forcing the relationship.

We can choose to obey the gospel or not.

> *Yet if any man suffer as a Christian, let him not be ashamed; but let him glorify God on this behalf. For the time is come that judgment must begin at the house of God: and if it first begin at us, what shall the end be*

of them that obey not the gospel of God (I Peter 4:16–17)?

Share the good news of salvation and pray that lost people will obey the gospel of God.

Man dies. *And all the days that Adam lived were nine hundred and thirty years: and he died* (Genesis 5:5). His descendants died. *And all the days of Seth were nine hundred and twelve years: and he died* (Genesis 5:8).

Methuselah lived longer than any other man, but he still died. *And all the days of Methuselah were nine hundred sixty and nine years: and he died* (Genesis 5:27). Everyone born after the Flood lived much shorter lives.

> *And the days of Terah were two hundred and five years: and Terah died in Haran (Genesis 11:32).*

> *And Sarah was an hundred and seven and twenty years old: these were the years of the life of Sarah (Genesis 23:1).*

So Joseph died, being an hundred and ten years old: and they embalmed him, and he was put in a coffin in Egypt (Genesis 50:26).

Man cannot conquer death. People have tried to avoid death by not thinking about it or doing whatever they could to stay healthy (as if ill health was the only cause of death). There are people who believed that if their dead, diseased body was immediately frozen, they could be brought back to life in the future when a cure for their disease was found. Man cannot conquer death, but Jesus conquered death. When Lazarus had been in the grave four days, Jesus came and proved He had power over death.

Jesus said, Take ye away the stone. Martha, the sister of him that was dead, saith unto him, Lord, by this time he stinketh: for he hath been dead four days. Jesus saith unto her, Said I not unto thee, that, if thou wouldest believe, thou shouldest see the glory of God? Then they took away the stone from the place where the dead was laid. And Jesus lifted up his eyes, and said, Father, I thank thee that thou hast heard me. And I knew that thou hearest me always: but because of the people which stand by I said it, that they may believe that thou hast sent me. And when he thus had spoken, he cried with a loud voice, Lazarus, come forth. And he that was dead came forth, bound hand and foot with graveclothes: and his face was bound about with a napkin. Jesus saith unto them, Loose him, and let him go (John 11:39–44).

That's power! Who else but the Almighty God could bring life to dead, rotting flesh? Eventually Lazarus did die again, but the day is coming when his body will be resurrected to die no more. *Behold, I shew you a mystery; We shall not all sleep, but shall all be changed, In a moment, in the twinkling of an eye, at the last trump: for the trumpet shall sound, and the dead shall be raised incorruptible, and we shall be changed* (I Corinthians 15:51–52). Every moment brings us closer to that glorious moment when the trumpet shall sound.

Knowledge of Sin

What is sin? One Hebrew word for *sin*[21] is *chattach* (khat-tawth'), which means "an offense." It is the sin of Sodom and Gomorrah.

> *And the LORD said, Because the cry of Sodom and Gomorrah is great, and because their sin is very grievous; I will go down now, and see whether they have done altogether according to the cry of it, which is come unto me; and if not, I will know (Genesis 18:20–21).*

Depravity, filthiness, and homosexuality were their *chattach*, or offense. God's punishment for their offense was sudden destruction.

> *Then the LORD rained upon Sodom and upon Gomorrah brimstone and fire from the LORD out of heaven; And he overthrew those cities, and all the plain, and all the inhabitants of the cities, and that which grew upon the ground (Genesis 19:24–25).*

The well-watered plains became a desert wasteland. Just as the worldwide flood left its mark on the earth, God's judgment on Sodom and Gomorrah left its mark, too. Everything burned.

Idol worship is another offense to God. While Moses was on Mount Sinai receiving the Ten Commandments, the Israelites demanded idols. Aaron made a golden calf for them to worship. Then Moses came down from the mount.

> *And it came to pass, as soon as he came nigh unto the camp, that he saw the calf, and the dancing: and Moses' anger waxed hot, and he cast the tables out of his hands, and brake them beneath the mount. And he took the calf which they had made, and burnt it in the fire, and ground it to powder, and strawed it upon the water, and made the children of Israel drink of it (Exodus 32:19–20).*

The punishment didn't end there. When Moses saw the Israelites were naked as they worshipped the calf, he said,

Who is on the LORD's side? let him come unto me. And all the sons of Levi gathered themselves together unto him. And he said unto them, Thus saith the LORD God of Israel, Put every man his sword by his side, and go in and out from gate to gate throughout the camp, and slay every man his brother, and every man his companion, and every man his neighbour. And the children of Levi did according to the word of Moses: and there fell of the people that day about three thousand men (Exodus 32:26b–28).

Moses interceded for the people because their offense was great. *And it came to pass on the morrow, that Moses said unto the people, Ye have sinned a great sin: and now I will go up unto the LORD; peradventure I shall make an atonement for your sin* (Exodus 32:30).

Moses asked for forgiveness for their sin, but the sin still had its penalty. *And the LORD plagued the people, because they made the calf, which Aaron made* (Exodus 32:35). God knew Aaron and the people were guilty of making the golden calf, so all of them suffered the consequences of the great sin of idol worship.

Chattach is the word used for sin offering throughout the Old Testament.

> *And the LORD spake unto Moses, saying, Speak unto Aaron and to his sons, saying, This is the law of the sin-offering: In the place where the burnt-offering is killed shall the sin-offering be killed before the LORD: it is most holy (Leviticus 6:24–25).*

Iniquity[22] is another word for sin and is translated from the Hebrew word *avon* or *avown* (aw-vone'), which means "perversity, evil." The wicked speak evil. *The words of his mouth are iniquity and deceit: he hath left off to be wise, and to do good* (Psalm 36:3). Notice the result of iniquity is a lack of wisdom and ceasing to do good.

Not doing God's commandments is iniquity. Because of iniquity, there was God-appointed terrors.

> *But if ye will not hearken unto me, and will not do all these commandments; And*

if ye shall despise my statutes, or if your soul abhor my judgments, so that ye will not do all my commandments, but that ye break my covenant: I also will do this unto you; I will even appoint over you terror, consumption, and the burning ague, that shall consume the eyes, and cause sorrow of heart: and ye shall sow your seed in vain, for your enemies shall eat it. [...] And ye shall perish among the heathen, and the land of your enemies shall eat you up. And they that are left of you shall pine away in their iniquity in your enemies' lands; and also in the iniquities of their fathers shall they pine away with them (Leviticus 26:14–16, 38–39).

Sickness and tough times are not always because of iniquity; however, when the Israelites ignored God's commandments, they suffered.

Thankfully, God pardons iniquity. *Bless the LORD, O my soul, and forget not all his benefits: Who forgiveth all thine iniquities; who healeth all thy diseases; Who redeemeth thy life from destruction*

(Psalm 103:2–4a). Hallelujah! The LORD God forgives all our iniquities. That's a tremendous gift.

The word *trespass*[23] is from the Hebrew word *asham* (aw-shawm'), which means "guilt" in many Old Testament verses. God commanded that the Israelites bring an offering to ask for forgiveness.

> *And the LORD spake unto Moses, saying, If a soul sin, and commit a trespass against the LORD, and lie unto his neighbour in that which was delivered him to keep, or in fellowship, or in a thing taken away by violence, or hath deceived his neighbour; Or have found that which was lost, and lieth concerning it, and sweareth falsely; in any of all these that a man doeth, sinning therein: Then it shall be, because he hath sinned, and is guilty, that he shall restore that which he took violently away, or the thing which he hath deceitfully gotten, or that which was delivered him to keep, or the lost thing which he found. Or all that about which he hath sworn falsely; he shall even restore it in the principal, and shall add the fifth part more thereto,*

*and give it unto him to whom it apper-
taineth, in the day of his trespass-offering
(Leviticus 6:1–5).*

Notice that the trespasses named are stealing,
deceiving, and lying. To clear himself from the guilt
of these trespasses against his neighbor, the sinner
was to restore his neighbor's goods or pay what the
stolen thing was worth with interest. To clear his
guilt before the LORD, the sinner was required to
bring a ram as a trespass-offering.

*And he shall bring his trespass-offering
unto the LORD, a ram without blemish
out of the flock, with thy estimation, for a
trespass-offering unto the priest: And the
priest shall make an atonement for him
before the LORD: and it shall be forgiven
him for any thing of all that he hath done
in trespassing therein (Leviticus 6:6–7).*

Jesus gave Himself as our ram by dying on the cross
of Calvary.

*And you, being dead in your sins and
the uncircumcision of your flesh, hath*

> *he quickened together with him, having forgiven you all trespasses; Blotting out the handwriting of ordinances that was against us, which was contrary to us, and took it out of the way, nailing it to his cross (Colossians 2:13–14).*

Because of Jesus, the perfect sacrifice, all our trespasses are forgiven. It's like the hymn *"My Sins Are Blotted Out, I Know!"* declares. When we want to be free of the heavy weight of guilt, we must look to the Lamb of God.

The word *transgression*[24] is the translation of the Hebrew word *pesha* (peh'-shah), which means "a revolt." This sin is rebellion against just authority. It's the willful breaking of God's law.

> *Now we know that what things soever the law saith, it saith to them who are under the law: that every mouth may be stopped, and all the world may become guilty before God. Therefore by the deeds of the law there shall no flesh be justified in his sight: for by the law is the knowledge of sin (Romans 3:19–20).*

Transgressors know God's commandments yet disobey them. Even partial obedience is disobedience. King Saul forfeited his position as king because he disobeyed God by not completely destroying the Amalekites.

> *And Samuel said, Hath the LORD as great delight in burnt-offerings and sacrifices, as in obeying the voice of the LORD? Behold, to obey is better than sacrifice, and to hearken than the fat of rams. For rebellion is as the sin of witchcraft, and stubbornness is as iniquity and idolatry. Because thou hast rejected the word of the LORD, he hath also rejected thee from being king (I Samuel 15:22–23).*

A transgressor loves arguing and fighting. It's the one who intentionally says and does things to make others upset. *He loveth transgression that loveth strife: and he that exalteth his gate seeketh destruction* (Proverbs 17:19). We know this to be true. When a certain person is absent, it's calm at the family gathering or at the work place. When that certain person arrives, strife begins. He loves getting others stirred up or upset. The scorner also stirs up strife. For example, a guest in your home expresses a low opinion of your hospitality by saying something like, "I can't believe this is all you have to offer." The only way to stop a scorner is to have him leave. *Cast out the scorner, and contention shall go out; yea, strife and reproach shall cease* (Proverbs 22:10). A transgressor enjoys strife and often starts the "revolt."

There is hope for transgressors. For years, my maternal grandfather instigated arguments about God and the Bible. He convinced himself that evolution was true and wouldn't acknowledge the Creator. On one visit, when Grandpa again challenged our belief in God, my husband asked Grandpa if there was any part of the Bible that he liked. Grandpa admitted that he did like Psalm 23. My husband said, "Good. Let me read it to you. 'The LORD is my shepherd.'" He looked at Grandpa and said, "He is not. 'I shall not want.' Yes, you will." As he read through the psalm, my husband kept this up. When he finished, my husband told Grandpa, "If you don't want the rest of the Bible, you don't get Psalm 23 either." Grandpa just nodded his head in agreement. We and other saved relatives kept witnessing and praying. As Grandpa got older, Alzheimer's disease began to set in, and he ended up in a local nursing home. John Wood from the Baptist church in the area held church services for the nursing home residents. He had known Grandpa for years and knew he was a transgressor. Grandpa had always liked music, and one day he heard the music from Mr. Wood's service. Grandpa sat down and listened to the hymns and the message. Afterward, he talked with Mr. Wood. Grandpa finally bowed his head and asked for forgiveness for his sins. After his salvation, Grandpa's favorite hymn was "*Amazing Grace.*" He didn't argue about God or the Bible anymore. Grandpa and John Wood are both with the Lord now, and what a joyous meeting it would have been.

> *A very precious verse about transgressions is Isaiah 43:25, which states, I, even I, am he that blotteth out thy transgressions for mine own sake, and will not remember thy sins.*

Knowledge of God's Word

Knowledge of God's Word wipes out assumptions. Assumptions are based on ignorance. They always get us into trouble. Without Knowledge of God's Word, it's easy to be misled. "Well, I just assumed they were telling the truth. They quoted Bible verses. I didn't know that they don't believe that Jesus is God."

We need to know what the Scriptures teach about Jesus to protect us from false teachings and cults because the Bible clearly tells us, *For many deceivers are entered into the world, who confess not that Jesus Christ is come in the flesh. This is a deceiver and an antichrist* (II John 7). The Jehovah Witnesses are in this group of deceivers. Remember that even Satan is called an angel of light.

> *For such are false apostles, deceitful workers, transforming themselves into the apostles of Christ. And no marvel; for Satan himself is transformed into an angel of light. Therefore it is no great thing if his ministers also be transformed as the ministers of righteousness; whose end shall be according to their works (II Corinthians 11:13–15).*

Ignorance is not bliss. We are to have Knowledge of God's Word for our own good. If we don't know whether we are being told the truth or not, we need to find out. "Assume the best" is not a command of God and is not taught in Scripture. It is the philosophy of the simple. *The simple believeth every word: but the prudent man looketh well to his going* (Proverbs 14:15).

Appearance can deceive us. Consider Joshua and the princes of the congregation of Israel when the Gibeonites, inhabitants of Canaan, arrived as false ambassadors.

> *And when the inhabitants of Gibeon heard what Joshua had done unto Jericho and to Ai, They did work wilily, and went and made as if they had been ambassadors, and took old sacks upon their asses, and wine bottles, old, and rent, and bound up; And old shoes and clouted upon their feet, and old garments upon them; and all the bread of their provision was dry and mouldy (Joshua 9:3–5).*

Their appearance supported their lie that they had come on a long journey to make a league with Israel.

> *And they said unto him [Joshua], From a very far country thy servants are come because of the name of the LORD thy God: for we have heard the fame of him, and all that he did in Egypt, And all that he did to the two kings of the Amorites, that were beyond Jordan, to Sihon king of Heshbon, and to Og king of Bashan, which was at Ashtaroth (Joshua 9:9–10).*

God knew who these men were, but neither Joshua nor the princes sought God for that Knowledge. Instead, they assumed the Gibeonites were telling the truth based on appearance.

> *And the men took of their victuals, and asked not counsel at the mouth of the LORD. And Joshua made peace with them, and made a league with them, to let them live: and the princes of the congregation sware unto them (Joshua 9:14–15).*

We need to know the truth about those who want us to sign a contract, support their campaign, or accept their religion. The Gibeonites worshipped idols, but said they came because of the name of the Lord their God. Having Knowledge of God's Word and seeking the Lord in prayer will guide us to the truth.

Knowledge of God's Word dispels doubts. "I doubt God can meet this need. This is a very large medical bill." Instead, Philippians 4:19 states, *But my God shall supply all your need according to his riches in glory by Christ Jesus.* Is God able? Does He keep His Word? Have you asked Him? *Ask, and it shall be given you; seek, and ye shall find; knock, and it shall be opened unto you* (Matthew 7:7). Jesus also said, *And whatsoever ye shall ask in my name, that will I do, that the Father may be glorified in the Son* (John 14:13). God is glorified in answering prayer, and His glory is for our good. There is great joy in knowing that our heavenly Father has heard us and answered. God's timing is perfect. *For my thoughts are not your thoughts, neither are your ways my ways, saith the LORD* (Isaiah 55:8).

"I don't think God cares about me" is another doubt that Knowledge of God's Word dispels. I Peter 5:7 states, *Casting all your care upon him; for he careth for you.* God cares because He says He does. *We love him, because he first loved us* (I John 4:19). The book of Psalms reveals the heart of God. Read it. I suggest having a box of tissues handy. He cares so much about you! *The LORD is nigh unto them that are of a broken heart; and saveth such as be of a contrite spirit. Many are the afflictions of the righteous: but the LORD delivereth him out of them all* (Psalm 34:18).

Knowledge of God's Word changes lives. *Blessed are they that keep his testimonies, and that seek him with the whole heart. They also do no iniquity: they walk in his ways* (Psalm 119:2–3). The apostle Paul admonished the young preacher, Timothy, to show how God changes young people. *Let no man despise thy youth; but be thou an example of the believers, in word, in conversation, in charity, in spirit, in faith, in purity* (I Timothy 4:12). Christianity is not a stagnant faith. It is a vital, growing Knowledge of the Lord Jesus Christ.

According as his divine power hath given unto us all things that pertain unto life and godliness, through the knowledge of him that hath called us to glory and virtue: Whereby are given unto us exceeding great and precious promises: that by these ye might be partakers of the divine nature, having escaped the corruption that is in the world through lust. And beside this, giving all diligence, add to your faith virtue; and to virtue knowledge; And to knowledge temperance; and to temperance patience; and to patience godliness; And to godliness brotherly kindness; and to brotherly kindness charity (II Peter 1:3–7).

Consider the things we are to be adding to our lives:

- Add faith. *But without faith is it impossible to please him: for he that cometh to God must believe that he is, and that he is a rewarder of them that diligently seek him* (Hebrews 11:6). The whole chapter of Hebrews 11 is a record of those who exhibited faith.

- Add virtue. Virtue[25] is "moral life and conduct; a particular moral excellence." For example, those with virtue really do believe and practice the adage *Honesty is the best policy.*

- Add Knowledge. *But grow in grace, and in the knowledge of our Lord and Saviour Jesus Christ. To him be glory both now and for ever. Amen* (II Peter 3:18). Faithfully reading God's Word, studying it, and memorizing verses is how to have Knowledge.

- Add temperance. Temperance[26] means "self-control" (notice the word *temper*) which would include self-control of appetite and other fleshly desires.

- Add patience. Patience[27] is "cheerful or hopeful endurance." This is the patience of Job. *Behold, we count them happy which endure. Ye have heard of the patience of Job, and have seen the end of the Lord; that the Lord is very pitiful, and of tender mercy* (James 5:11). Job enjoyed all the blessings that came after he endured suffering. *So the*

LORD blessed the latter end of Job more than his beginning (Job 42:12a).

- Add godliness. *Because it is written, Be ye holy; for I am holy* (I Peter 1:16). Daniel in the Old Testament is an example of someone who had added godliness to his life. He wouldn't defile himself with the king of Babylon's meat and wine and faithfully prayed to God three times a day. Study the life of Daniel. It is possible to live in a sinful world and be godly.

- Add brotherly kindness. *Be kindly affectioned one to another with brotherly love; in honour preferring one another* (Romans 12:10). It's letting someone else have his preference instead of insisting on our own preference.

- Add charity. *Let all your things be done with charity* (I Corinthians 16:14). Charity[28] is translated from the Greek word for love, which is *agape* (ag-ah'-pay). It's defined in Ephesians 5:2 *And walk in love, as Christ also hath loved us, and hath given himself for us an offering and a sacrifice to God for a sweetsmelling savour.* Charity is Christ's love for us. It's the love that made Him willing to go to the cross and be the sacrifice for our sins.

- Adding faith, virtue, knowledge, temperance, patience, godliness, brotherly kindness, and charity to our lives increases our Knowledge of Jesus Christ. *For if these things be in you, and abound, they make you that ye shall neither be barren nor unfruitful in the knowledge of our Lord Jesus Christ* (II Peter 1:8).

As we're growing in the Knowledge of Jesus Christ, it shows. Think of an apple tree. How do we know it is growing? Well, it gets taller, produces green leaves, brings forth blossoms, and finally, apples. We recognize an apple tree because it has the characteristics of an apple tree and produces apples. As we grow spiritually, the character of Christ will be seen. Besides those things listed above, we will have the fruit of the Spirit defined in Galatians 5:22-23: love, joy, peace, longsuffering, gentleness, goodness, faith, meekness, and temperance. It identifies us as children of God.

Knowledge of God's Word brings forth more fruit. *The sower soweth the word. […] And these are they which are sown on good ground; such as hear the word, and receive it, and bring forth fruit, some thirtyfold, some sixty, and some an hundred* (Mark 4:14, 20).

This can't be referring to the fruit of the Spirit given in Galatians 5:22–23 since only nine are listed. The fruit from the work of the sower is other Christians. For example, when we plant a kernel of corn, a cornstalk grows. On that cornstalk grows a cob of corn. On the cob are many kernels of corn. These are planted, and more cornstalks grow. Each of these cornstalks produce many cobs of corn. The many cobs of corn have hundreds of kernels of corn, and just as corn produces more corn, Christians should produce more Christians.

When Adoniram Judson, a Baptist missionary in Burma, began his ministry, one soul trusted Christ. As time passed, a few more trusted Christ. Those folks started telling others about Christ, and more folks trusted Christ. Hundreds of Burmese people came to faith in Jesus, and it started with one. The sower keeps scattering seed because his goal is to have a harvest. God desires a harvest of souls and calls us to be His sowers. *He that goeth forth and weepeth, bearing precious seed, shall doubtless come again with rejoicing, bringing his sheaves with him* (Psalm 126:6).

Lack of Knowledge

Deficiencies are detrimental. For example, vitamin C deficiency results in scurvy. Low potassium affects the heart, muscles, and nerves. Even lack of dark chocolate may result in low iron. Any volunteers for a study to prove it? Seriously, low iron causes anemia. A deficiency or lack of Knowledge is also detrimental. *Also, that the soul be without knowledge, it is not good; and he that hasteth with his feet sinneth* (Proverbs 19:2). Lack of Knowledge leads to the destruction of a nation's people. The prophet Hosea wrote:

Hear the word of the LORD, ye children of Israel: for the LORD hath a controversy with the inhabitants of the land, because there is no truth, nor mercy, nor knowledge of God in the land. [...] My people are destroyed for lack of knowledge: because thou hast rejected knowledge, I will also reject thee, that thou shalt be no priest to me: seeing thou hast forgotten the law of thy God, I will also forget thy children. As they were increased, so they sinned against me: therefore will I change their glory into shame (Hosea 4:1,6–7).

Because Israel had forgotten God, they had no Knowledge of God. They sinned against Him by worshipping idols. God let them be destroyed by sword, famine, and pestilence. The book of Judges is a record of generations in Israel that followed a continuous cycle from lack of Knowledge of God. They forsook the Lord, served idols, and suffered in the hands of their enemies. They cried to the Lord for deliverance, He raised up a deliverer, then when the judge died, they forsook the Lord again, served idols, and on it went.

There are nations today that have no Knowledge of God, and consequently they sin against God and worship idols. Buddhism is the leading religion in China today. Chinese history is a sad story of natural disasters (acts of God), poverty, and oppression. In India, Hindus make up the majority of the population. India is among the poorer countries of the world. Arab nations practice Islam. They bow before the false god Allah. Their religion teaches violence and death. They may carry a metal sword, but we can wield *the sword of the Spirit, which is the word of God* (Ephesians 6:17b).

Go, or support someone who will go and reach out with the Knowledge of God. These nations need Bibles. They need to hear the good news of salvation whether it's through literature, radio, street preaching, door-to-door soul winning, or even social media.

There are people in the United States who have never heard the name of Jesus—except maybe as a swear word. They need to be reached as well. Even the elderly can get involved. Peggy is a senior citizen who has breathing problems. When her transportation arrives to take her to the doctor, she hands the driver a tract. She leaves tracts by the same old magazines in the waiting room. Whenever Peggy has been admitted to the hospital, she has a stack of tracts with her to give the nurses, cleaning staff, or whoever. She does what she can to get the Knowledge of God out to those around her.

Recently a gas station attendant asked me, "How are you today?"

I answered, "Oh, God is so good to me! I wish everyone could know God as I know Him. Here, this will tell you about Him. Have a great day!"

The girl accepted the tract. We should all care enough to share the Knowledge of God!

Further Study for Knowledge

Knowledge of God

1. *Jehovah-Jireh*[29] (je-hoe'-vah yeer'-eh) means "Jehovah provides." Read Genesis 22:1–14.
    a. Who used this name for God?
    b. What did God provide?

2. *Jehovah-Rophe*[30] (je-hoe'-vah ro'-fay) means "Jehovah heals." Read Exodus 15:23–26.
    a. What was wrong at Marah?
    b. How was the problem solved?

3. *Jehovah-Nissi*[31] (je-hoe'-vah nis'-see) means "Jehovah, my banner." For Israel in the wilderness,

the banner was Moses' rod. *Jehovah-Nissi* refers to the Lord as being lifted up. Read Exodus 17:8–16 and Deuteronomy 20:1–4.

   a. Who was the enemy?

   b. Who would fight for Israel?

Knowledge of Man

4. What did Jabal dwell in and what did he raise (Genesis 4:20)?

5. What did Jubal invent (Genesis 4:21)?

6. What metals did Tubal-cain use (Genesis 4:22)?

7. What does this reveal about man before the Flood?

Knowledge of Sin

8. Fill in the blanks to complete the Ten Commandments given in Exodus 20:1–17.

I. Thou shalt have _____ other gods _____ me.

II. Thou shalt not _____
thee any _____ _____.

III. Thou shalt not take the _____ of the
Lord thy God in _____.

IV. Remember the _____ day, to
keep it _____.

V. _____ thy father and thy mother.

VI. Thou shalt not _____.

VII. Thou shalt not _____.

IX. Thou shalt
not bear _____ _____.

X. Thou shalt not _____.

Knowledge of God's Word

9. How is God's Word described in Hebrews 4:12?

10. According to Joshua 1:8, when are we to meditate on God's Word?

Pillar #4

Understanding

The fear of the LORD is the beginning of wisdom: and the knowledge of the holy is understanding Proverbs 9:10.

Fear of the LORD allows us to hear Instruction, receive Knowledge, and get Understanding. *Wisdom is the principal thing; therefore get wisdom: and with all thy getting get understanding* (Proverbs 4:7).

To get Understanding, we must go to the source of Understanding. *For the LORD giveth wisdom: out of his mouth cometh knowledge and understanding* (Proverbs 2:6). Understanding comes from God Himself.

Understanding and Talents

Think about what we call talents or God-given abilities. When King Solomon was determined to build the temple of the Lord in Jerusalem, he asked Huram, king of Tyre, to send a man skilled in working with metal and wood.

> *Then Huram the king of Tyre answered in writing, which he sent to Solomon, Because the LORD hath loved his people, he hath made thee king over them. Huram said moreover, Blessed be the LORD God of Israel, that made heaven and earth, who hath given to David the king a wise son, endued with prudence and understanding, that might build an house for the LORD, and an house for his kingdom. And now I have sent a cunning man, endued with understanding, of Huram my father's. The son of a woman of the daughters of Dan, and his father was a man of Tyre, skillful to work in gold, and in silver, in brass, in iron, in stone, and in timber, in purple, in blue, and in fine linen, and in crimson; also to grave any manner of graving, and to find*

out every device which shall be put to him, with thy cunning men, and with the cunning men of my lord David thy father (II Chronicles 2:11–14).

First, Solomon had Understanding. He knew the temple should be glorious; therefore, he needed skilled workmen—those who would do the job right and well. It's like needing a new roof on the house. Do we hire just anybody who is willing to get up on a roof or do we seek a skilled, honest roofer? Understanding seeks for the latter. Second, Huram sent a man who had Understanding. He had the skill and the ability to work with all kinds of metals, stone, wood, and linen. He may have been taught by his father, but his Understanding of building materials and techniques still came from God.

What talents or abilities seem to come naturally for you? There are people that God has gifted with the skill to decorate beautifully, arrange hair, match colors and patterns, or organize things. The blind girl Fanny Crosby started writing poetry as a child. In her lifetime she wrote thousands of hymns; many are still being sung today. Dorcas in Acts 9 was skilled in sewing and used that talent to minister to the needy. She understood how to make clothing.

School subjects require Understanding. Daniel and his three friends had Understanding in science, language, and all learning. Daniel was also given Understanding in visions and dreams.

> As for these four children, God gave them knowledge and skill in all learning and wisdom: and Daniel had understanding in all visions and dreams. Now at the end of the days that the king had said he should bring them in, then the prince of the eunuchs brought them in before Nebuchadnezzar. And the king communed with them; and among them all was found none like Daniel, Hananiah, Mishael, and Azariah: therefore stood they before the king. And in all matters of wisdom and understanding, that the king enquired of them, he found them ten times better than all the magicians and astrologers that were in all his realm (Daniel 1:17–20).

These young men had wisdom and Understanding because they sought God. Godly youth can have ten times more wisdom and Understanding than older folks who do not have Knowledge of the holy. Proverbs 9:6 states, *Forsake the foolish, and live; and go in the way of understanding.*

I had to take Chemistry when I was in high school. Class went fine until we had to combine formulas on paper. The process didn't make sense to me. My teacher stayed after school a few nights a week to help some of us, and after two months, it clicked. I suddenly understood how the formulas worked. You know how it is; the light comes on. By the way, it was during that two months that I was saved. God then gave me Understanding. He even allowed me to get the highest grade on the chemistry final exam, beating the straight A student in the class. Having Understanding made the difference.

In what areas do we need Understanding? God provides Understanding to missionaries who must learn to speak foreign languages. Gladys Alward, for example, was dismissed from a missionary training center because the administration said she would be too old to learn Chinese by the time she finished. God wanted her in China, so she paid her own way and went. Gladys had a talent for hearing and speaking different English accents, such as cockney and Oxford. When she went to China, her natural talent for mimicking not only helped her learn Chinese, but speak it like a native.

Understanding was given to George Washington Carver, an American scientist. He was a talented botanist. Young George had a natural interest in plants and wanted to know all he could about them. He studied plants, learned how to use laboratory equipment, and, years later, he asked God what could be made from the peanut. He created hundreds of products from that legume, which helped Southern farmers—peanuts became a cash crop. He said, "There is literally nothing that I ever asked to do, that I asked the blessed Creator help me to do, that I have not been able to accomplish."[32] Mr. Carver understood that it was God who created the plants and gave him wisdom to make great things like peanut butter.

God will even give Understanding for fixing a meal with what we have on hand in the refrigerator and cupboard. With knowledge of flavor combinations and cooking techniques, we can gain Understanding of what we can make. Not every cook can just throw ingredients together and make them taste good. Understanding makes me realize that I need a cookbook to make most dishes, even a simple one like meatloaf. Thank you, Betty Crocker.

Understanding and Timing

Knowing the right time is Understanding. For example, when we were at a family gathering years ago with relatives who were believers and unbelievers, a saved family member brought up a doctrinal issue at the dinner table to start an argument with my husband. Wisely, my husband didn't take the bait and changed the topic. Later, his mother thanked him for his restraint. A family celebration wasn't the time to debate differing beliefs. (My husband grew up in an Italian family where there was no such thing as quiet discussions.) Understanding shows restraint and waits for the right time to address an issue.

Queen Esther had Understanding as well. She knew her husband, King Xerxes, liked his wine and admired her beauty. When Haman, a trusted high government official, planned to kill all the Jews, Esther didn't just get out of bed one morning, march into the throne room, and yell, "Xerxes, I've got to talk to you. Haman is plotting to kill me and all the rest of the Jews. You must stop this decree." She knew the king had to be approached at the right time in order for her request to be granted. Esther took time to prepare a banquet. She took time to don her most beautiful apparel. She did what she could to gain Xerxes's favor, but Esther's trust was in God and His timing. She fasted and prayed for three days before appearing in the throne room. Understanding waits on God. *My soul, wait thou only upon God; for my expectation is from him* (Psalm 62:5). This reminds me of the song "*Always Take Time to Pray.*"

By the way, you need to read the book of Esther aloud, in a group, some time. Every time the names Esther and Mordecai are read aloud, clap and cheer. When the name Haman is spoken, boo and hiss. I'm told that this is an actual Jewish custom during the feast of Purim.

Abigail, wife of Nabal, was also a woman of Understanding. In I Samuel 25:2–3, this husband and wife are described:

> *And there was a man in Maon, whose possessions were in Carmel; and the man was very great, and he had three thousand sheep, and a thousand goats: and he was shearing his sheep in Carmel. Now the name of the man was Nabal; and the name of his wife Abigail: and she was a woman of good understanding, and of a beautiful countenance: but the man was churlish and evil in his doings; and he was of the house of Caleb.*

First, Nabal was wealthy. Nothing wrong with having wealth; Abraham and his son Isaac possessed great flocks and herds. However, while Abraham was a man of justice and judgment, Nabal was churlish. This second description reveals Nabal's character. The word *churlish* means cruel, hard-hearted, and stubborn. Third, being evil in his doings put Nabal right up there with crooked car salesmen. Couldn't you imagine him selling a blind sheep to an unsuspecting shepherd? Finally, Nabal is identified as a son of Belial which is a man of worthlessness, akin to Satan. One of his servants told Abigail, *He is such a son of Belial, that a man cannot speak to him* (1 Samuel 25:17c).

Servant: "Master, David and his men are—"

Nabal (interrupting): "What do I care? Get back to work. I don't want to hear any more about David."

What the servant wanted to tell Nabal was that David and four hundred armed men were coming because Nabal had rudely refused David's request for a portion of the abundant sheepshearer's feast. The servant then went to Abigail.

Only two descriptions of Abigail are given; she was beautiful and had good Understanding. The servant knew that she would listen.

> *Servant: Behold, David sent messengers out of the wilderness to salute our master; and he railed on them. But the men were very good unto us, and we were not hurt, neither missed we any thing, as long as we were conversant with them, when we were*

in the fields: They were a wall unto us both by night and day, all the while we were with them keeping the sheep. Now therefore know and consider what thou wilt do; for evil is determined against our master, and against all his household: for he is such a man of Belial, that a man cannot speak to him (1 Samuel 25:14b–17).

There wasn't time to fast and pray. There wasn't time to don her most beautiful apparel or even brush her hair. Abigail understood it was time to act. With haste, she took two hundred loaves, two bottles of wine, five ready-to-eat sheep, five measures of parched corn, one hundred clusters of raisins, and two hundred cakes of figs and sent it all to David. (This was the start of fast food delivery. Gentiles later changed the menu to sausage pizza delivered in a cardboard box.) Abigail rode after the servants. Understanding of the situation and timing made her realize that the sight of food had to come first. No amount of words takes the place of a good meal when people are hungry.

When Abigail met David, she fell to the ground, bowed down, and said, *I pray thee, forgive the trespass of thine handmaid: for the LORD will certainly make my lord a sure house; because my lord fighteth the battles of the LORD, and evil hath not been found in thee all thy days* (I Samuel 25:28). Abigail is a tremendous example of Understanding. First, she sent food, which met the immediate need. Second, she asked forgiveness, which calmed David's anger. Third, she reminded David that he was fighting the Lord's battles, which brought memories of victories. And lastly, she found him free of evil, which meant he was the opposite of Nabal and would do the right thing. David accepted the food and the apology. The crisis was over.

When Abigail returned home, she found Nabal feasting like a king. He was very drunk, so she understood that it was not the time to tell Nabal what had happened. Understanding made her realize that she would have to wait until Nabal was sober; it's difficult to reason with a drunkard. *But it came to pass in the morning, when the wine was gone out of Nabal, and his wife had told him these things, that his heart died within him, and he became as a stone. And it came to pass about ten days after, that the LORD smote Nabal, and he died* (I Samuel 25:37–38). When David heard of Nabal's death, he was very thankful that he had not avenged himself. He then asked Abigail to be his wife, and she accepted. *Good understanding giveth favour: but the way of transgressors is hard* (Proverbs 13:15). God then blessed her with a son, Chileab, David's second son according to II Samuel 3:3. Doing things at the right time makes all the difference.

Understanding and Tantrums

When our daughter, Rebecca, was about two years old, she began having what we thought were temper tantrums. She would start kicking and screaming for no apparent reason. Discipline didn't help. Extra attention didn't help. Ignoring the tantrum didn't help. Finally, one Sunday, on the way home from church as Rebecca started screaming in her car seat, I asked God what was wrong with our little girl. He brought one word to mind—chocolate. My sister had told me her son, who was the same age as Rebecca, was allergic to chocolate. I asked relatives and people at church not to give her any more chocolate. No more chocolate, no more tantrums. Problem solved. On my own, I never would have suspected a food allergy to be the cause of a "behavior problem." Please take people seriously when a parent, a spouse, or the person himself says that he can't have certain foods or beverages, including dairy products, coffee, or even chocolate. Allergic reactions may be far worse than a rash. Finding the root cause of a tantrum or problem is the work of Understanding.

Do you know why Moses struck the rock twice in the desert of Zin instead of speaking to it as God commanded? *And the LORD spake unto Moses saying, Take the rod, and gather thou the assembly together, thou, and Aaron thy brother, and speak ye unto the rock before their eyes; and it shall give forth his water, and thou shalt bring forth to them water out of the rock: so thou shalt give the congregation and their beasts drink* (Numbers 20:7–8). It was a simple command. Why then didn't Moses do as God said? *And Moses lifted up his hand, and with his rod he smote the rock twice: and the water came out abundantly, and the congregation drank, and their beasts also* (Numbers 20:11). One would think that Moses struck the rock out of frustration; he did call the children of Israel rebels as they gathered before the rock. *And Moses and Aaron gathered the congregation together before the rock, and he said unto them, Hear now, ye rebels; must we fetch you water out of this rock* (Numbers 20:10)? Anger and frustration would seem to be the cause for Moses' disobedience to God's command, but God tells us the root cause. *And the LORD spake unto Moses and Aaron, Because ye believed me not, to sanctify me in the eyes of the children of Israel, therefore ye shall not bring this congregation into the land which I have given them* (Numbers 20:12). Moses and Aaron did not believe God and disbelief cost them going into the land that God promised to Abraham.

Do we believe what God tells us? Speaking to a rock to supply water for all the children of Israel does not make sense, but that was God's command. Yes, God met their need for water when Moses struck the rock, but He had so much more for Moses and Aaron. Is disbelief the root cause that is holding us back from God's blessings?

Besides food allergies and disbelief, the root cause of tantrums or aggressive behavior can range from a sense of injustice, hopelessness, or the fear, shame, and guilt of being abused. Tantrums could also just be the outcome of the lack of discipline. Understanding looks behind the obvious tantrum and seeks the hidden cause. As Psalm 119:169 says,

*Let my cry come near before thee, O LORD: give me
understanding according to thy word.*

Understanding and Treasure

Understanding has great value. We may work hard to
obtain money and possessions, but Understanding
is better than riches. *How much better is it to
get wisdom than gold! and to get understanding
rather to be chosen than silver* (Proverbs 16:16)!
Exclamation points are not common in Scripture,
so, obviously, they are alerting us to get the point
(pun intended) that wisdom and Understanding
are great. When prospectors found gold or silver,
they got excited. "Gold! I found gold!" Likewise,
receiving Understanding should fill us with the
excitement of discovery.

Hiero, king of the ancient Greek city of Syracuse,
decided to have a magnificent crown made. He
weighed a precise amount of gold and then commanded a goldsmith to fashion a laurel wreath
crown using all the gold, and only gold. The goldsmith took the gold, and on the appointed day, he
presented Hiero with an exquisite crown. The weight

of the crown equaled the amount of gold given, so the king was pleased and paid the goldsmith.

After some time, Hiero heard rumors that the goldsmith substituted another metal for part of the gold, cheating the king. The wise king would not accuse the goldsmith based on rumors, but he did want to know the truth. Did the goldsmith cheat him or not? How could the amount of gold in the crown be tested without damaging the crown in any way? The king called for twenty-two-year-old Archimedes—a Greek mathematician, scientist, and engineer—to solve the problem.

Archimedes admitted he didn't know a way to prove if the crown was pure gold or not without damaging the crown, but he would think about it. He was thinking about the crown when he went to the public baths. As he lowered himself into the tub of water, he noticed that water spilled over the sides of the tub. The lower his body sank, the more water spilled out. The volume of his body displaced an equal volume of water. Without stopping to put on his clothes, Archimedes ran from the bath house yelling, "Eureka, Eureka!" which means "I have found it! I have found it!" (The Greek people would not have been as shocked as we might think to see a nude runner. They probably thought Archimedes was an Olympic athlete since nudity was common at the ancient Olympic games.)

Archimedes found the answer to the king's problem. *"If the weight of the water displaced is less than the weight of the object, the object will sink. Otherwise the object will float, with the weight of the water displaced equal to the weight of the object."*[33] That became Archimedes' Principle. Simply put, the size (volume) of an object and its weight (density) will determine how deep it will sink in fluid, such as water. As the object sinks, it forces water out in an equal amount. For example, if a bucket of water is filled to the brim, placing a brick of cork will barely force any water out of the bucket because cork floats, but placing a brick of gold in the bucket will force water out because it sinks to the bottom. Understanding helped Archimedes realize that a pure gold crown would be smaller (have less volume) than a crown of mixed metals of the same weight because gold is heavier than silver; therefore, a crown of gold mixed with silver would force out more water. Archimedes proved that the goldsmith had cheated the king. The greater treasure than the gold was Understanding how to reveal the truth about the crown.

When we get Understanding of the truths found in God's Word, we could yell, "Praise God" or "Thank you, Lord!" or even "Eureka!" *Happy is the man that findeth wisdom, and the man that getteth understanding* (Proverbs 3:13).

When we have Understanding, we can move forward with confidence. Difficult tasks become easy, mysteries of God are made clear, and things work out for the best.

Further Study for Understanding

Look up the verses from Psalm 119 to answer the questions.

1. How do we receive Understanding? (Psalm 119:104)

2. What can we learn from Understanding? (Psalm 119:73)

3. What can we know from Understanding? (Psalm 119:125)

4. Who can receive Understanding? (Psalm 119:130)

5. What did the psalmist say when he received Understanding? (Psalm 119:144)

6. What promise did the psalmist make when he received Understanding? (Psalm 119:34)

Pillar #5

Discretion

*A good man sheweth favour,and lendeth:
he will guide his affairs with discretion
(Psalm 112:5).*

Discretion is translated from five different Hebrew words. For the above verse and Isaiah 28:26, *Discretion*[34] would be from the word *mishpat* (mish-pawt') meaning "a verdict (favorable or unfavorable) pronounced judicially; a judgment." This is the meaning used for the pillar of Discretion. The word *judgment* is a legal term. Evidence is presented in court, then the judge makes a decision. Discretion would consider Fear of the LORD, Instruction, Knowledge, and Understanding, then make a judgment.

A farmer is a good example of Discretion.

> *Doth the plowman plow all day to sow? doth he open and break the clods of his ground? When he hath made plain the face thereof, doth he not cast abroad the fitches, and scatter the cummin, and cast in the principal wheat and the appointed barley and the rie in their place? For his God doth instruct him to discretion, and doth teach him (Isaiah 28:24–26).*

The farmer who has Discretion knows that at a certain season of the year it's time to plant. Before he can sow seed, he must ready the field. The soil has to be broken up and raked smooth. At the right time, the different crops are planted. The plowman has checked soil, seed quality, planting instructions, equipment, and weather conditions. Good judgment results in a good crop.

The same is true in our lives. When we have readied our hearts to receive Fear of the LORD, Instruction, Knowledge, and Understanding, the good crop of Discretion will grow. We will have checked God's

Word, followed His Instruction, waited on His timing, and heeded His warnings.

Warning signs are posted in many places. Fencing around an electric facility has a sign that warns of the danger of electric shock and death. A sign on a road block reads "WARNING: Bridge Out Ahead." (Translation: You can't get there from here.) A label on a prescription warns that the medication can cause drowsiness, and you should not drive or operate machinery. ("Honey, we'll have to eat out tonight. The medication I'm taking warns that I should not operate machinery, so being at the stove would be dangerous. I'll get my coat.)

People do not come with warning signs, but Discretion will beware of the false friend, the fool, and the flatterer.

Beware of the False Friend

The false friend is the one who speaks kindly but is not loyal or trustworthy. It's the mentality of Judas Iscariot. He physically followed Jesus, but his heart was not with Him. When Mary of Bethany anointed

Jesus' feet with expensive ointment, Judas protested, seemingly as a friend of the poor.

> *Then saith one of his disciples, Judas Iscariot, Simon's son, which should betray him, Why was not this ointment sold for three hundred pence, and given to the poor? This he said, not that he cared for the poor; but because he was a thief, and had the bag, and bare what was put therein (John 12:4–6).*

Judas was a thief who later betrayed Jesus. He was a false friend.

By observing others, Discretion can compare their words to their actions. Is what they're saying supported by what they're doing? It has been said that your walk talks louder than your talk talks. A false friend eventually does something that reveals his or her real character and motives. The prodigal son discovered he had false friends when his money ran out. *And when he had spent all, there arose a mighty famine in that land; and he began to be in want* (Luke 15:14). When he was in want, his so-called friends didn't help him. *And he went and joined himself to a citizen of that country; and he sent him into his fields to feed swine. And he would fain have filled his belly with the husks that the swine did eat: and no man gave unto him* (Luke 15:15–16). They loved his money not him.

A false friend manipulates by stirring up anger or fear. It's the coworker who angrily complains about the job, the boss, the pay, the lunchroom, even the parking lot, and provokes others to complain as well. God commands, *Do all things without murmurings and disputings* (Philippians 2:14). That includes a job. Stirring up anger at work may be a way to hide laziness. "If others are upset and not getting the job done, no one will notice that I'm being careless or neglectful." In any case, the false friend who stirs up anger certainly hinders the work; the forward pace is slowed down or stopped completely. The false friend is a troublemaker.

Provoking people to anger not only causes trouble, it is dangerous; it incites a crowd to violence. When Paul was in Lystra, unbelieving Jews from Antioch and Iconium came and stirred up anger against the apostle.

And there came thither certain Jews from Antioch and Iconium, who persuaded the people, and, having stoned Paul, drew him out of the city, supposing he had been dead. Howbeit, as the disciples stood round about him, he rose up, and came into the city: and the next day he departed with Barnabas to Derbe (Acts 14:19–20).

Discretion knows not to make friends with someone who stirs up anger. *Make no friendship with an angry man; and with a furious man thou shalt not go: Lest thou learn his ways, and get a snare to thy soul* (Proverbs 22:24–25).

The false friend is the neighbor who knows Joanna is afraid of the dark and tells her stories to frighten her. "But Mommy, Eva May told me that hobgoblins hide under the bed and come out when it's dark." Eva May's scary story captured the little girl's imagination, so she was fearful. God tells us, *Casting down imaginations, and every high thing that exalteth itself against the knowledge of God, and bringing into captivity every thought to the obedience of Christ* (II Corinthians 10:5). A false friend manipulates by stirring up fear.

As adults, do we listen to and believe scary stories rather than trust in the Lord? As it neared the turn of the twenty-first century, the year 2000 A.D, the public was bombarded with reports that all computer systems would fail, and nothing would work. People panicked. Scammers and false friends saw an opportunity to make money off people's fears and sold survival kits at high prices. It was almost midnight on December 31, 1999. The countdown in Times Square began: 10...9...8...7...6...5...4...3...2...1...Happy New Year! Everything still worked. Feelings of fear became feelings of embarrassment. Generators and survival supplies were either stored away, given away, or sold at cheap prices. When we have Discretion, we trust in the Lord. *It is better to trust in the LORD than to put confidence in man* (Psalm 118:8). Without Discretion, we trust the wrong person.

Beware of the Fool

Discretion knows and understands how to respond to the fool. *Answer not a fool according to his folly, lest thou also be like unto him* (Proverbs 26:4). For example, Mrs. Heady brags about her beautiful flower garden and how she will definitely win first place at the fair again this year. Discretion does not say, "Oh, yeah? Wait 'til the judges see my double-bearded irises. Mine are the most beautiful in the county." That would be acting like Mrs. Heady. Instead, Discretion knows that it's wiser to be quiet and let Mrs. Heady go on bragging. Pride would eventually be Mrs. Heady's downfall.

Proverbs 26:5 states, *Answer a fool according to his folly, lest he be wise in his own conceit.* For example, Mrs. Conceit says, "I know there is no god." Discretion asks, "Do you know everything? Could it be that God exists in the percentage you don't know?" In this case, man's wisdom should be challenged. When my husband's older brother, Lou, was in the Air Force, a Mormon came on base to talk to the men. Seeing a crowd, Lou walked over to listen. The Mormon had a wide board and a narrow board for his illustration and was saying, "The problem with the Bible is that you can make it say whatever you want it to say." He then nailed one end of the narrow board to the wide board and twisted it back and forth. "The Book of Mormon stabilizes the Bible." The Mormon then nailed the other end of the narrow board to the wide board so it wouldn't move.

Lou, who was not saved at the time, spoke up, "That's not true. If you take a nail and pound it into the center of the board deep enough, the board won't move." The men listening began to think, realized Lou was right, and left. By the way, Lou trusted Jesus as his Saviour after his four years in the military. Discretion answers a fool according to his folly by challenging the fool to think. Is what you are saying really true? Someone says, "I only trust myself." Really? Do you have a perfect memory? As for me, I can't remember what I had for supper last night, and I made the meal!

Discretion can answer a fool because she seeks truth. She does this by gathering evidence: asking questions, verifying information, and searching God's Word.

Asking appropriate questions is part of good judgment. Teachers ask questions to determine if students are learning. "Can anyone tell me where the country of Turkey is located?" Employers ask questions to decide who to hire. "What experience or skills do you have?" Doctors ask questions to make a diagnosis. "How long have you had this condition?" With knowledge and understanding of the body and diseases, they can make a better judgment. Would we really want a doctor to diagnose us without asking questions?

Discretion verifies information. When the women told the disciples that Jesus had risen from the dead, Peter and John ran to the tomb. They had the opportunity to also be eyewitnesses that the tomb was indeed empty. Even better was seeing the risen Lord for themselves.

> *Then the same day at evening, being the first day of the week, when the doors were shut where the disciples were assembled for fear of the Jews, came Jesus and stood in the midst, and saith unto them, Peace be unto you. And when he had so said, he shewed unto them his hands and his side. Then were the disciples glad, when they saw the Lord (John 20:19–20).*

The disciples knew He was Jesus. He showed them His wounded hands and His pierced side. They could verify what Mary Magdalene and the other women had said: "He is risen!" The report of eye-witnesses can verify information.

Verifying information could even save a life. My mother-in-law was a member of a community club, Friendly Neighbors, that met every other week. At one meeting, they noticed a neighbor who attended every meeting hadn't come or called. Some of the members assumed she had just forgotten, but one went to her home the next day to see her. The woman had fallen and couldn't get to the phone. She got the help she needed because someone wanted to make sure she was okay. The neighbor's only regret was that she hadn't checked sooner. Discretion is aware when something is wrong, perhaps thinking, "That's just not like her." Discretion verifies whether something is wrong or not.

Discretion searches the Scriptures. What does God's Word say? What biblical principles apply here? She compares one scripture verse with another and doesn't look for a verse that fits her own ideas. Studying the Scriptures will bring us to truth.

When Paul and Silas were sent away from Thessalonica for their own safety, they found Jews in Berea willing to search the Scriptures.

> *And the brethren immediately sent away Paul and Silas by night unto Berea: who coming thither went into the synagogue of the Jews. These were more noble than those in Thessalonica, in that they received the word with all readiness of mind, and searched the scriptures daily, whether those things were so. Therefore many of them believed; also of honourable women which were Greeks, and of men, not a few (Acts 17:10–11).*

There was a willingness to hear God's Word, time spent studying God's Word, and belief resulted.

Beware of the Flatterer

Discretion recognizes the flatterer. It's the flatterer at the Dollar General store who greets you in an aisle by saying, "Hi, beautiful." This happened to me not long ago. I told him, "Well, my *husband* thinks so and that's all that matters." I turned down another aisle and avoided him. He tried it next on the young cashier. She wasn't fooled either. This kind of flatterer is not interested in a particular woman for her personality, beliefs, or character; rather, he is after any woman who will give him attention.

It's the salesman who says, "I can see you're an intelligent woman who knows a great bargain." Watch out! The bargain will be his choice at his price.

It's the woman always looking for sympathy who says, "I like talking to you. You really listen. Other people won't listen to me." She doesn't tell you that her sob story is the same one she's been telling for years. People got tired of hearing it all the time. Discretion knows the message of the sob story is "these are the reasons you must feel sorry for me and excuse whatever I do or say. I can't help being this way." (Almost sounds like a hound dog-howling country song.) Her sympathizers take up the mantra, "She can't help being that way. Let her do what she wants."

Discretion is not fooled by any of these flatterers because she has Fear of the LORD. Every flatterer appeals to Pride and Arrogancy. You're beautiful;

you're intelligent; you're a better listener than anyone else. Beware! Flattery is the bait to draw us into a snare. The snare can be a wrong relationship, a foolish purchase, or an emotional merry-go-round.

Nancy's Note: The following section is God's lesson to me on Discretion and the next pillars, Counsel and Reproof. Just as anyone who has taught the Bible knows, God sometimes allows a trial in our lives to teach us the lesson firsthand. After I had prayed about it for months, God made it clear that this trial was not just for my sake.

There's a sister in Christ who needs to hear what God did for me because He wants you to know that He will do the same for you. God knows all about the trial and will comfort you, too.

> *Blessed be God, even the Father of our LORD Jesus Christ, the Father of mercies, and the God of all comfort; Who comforteth us in all our tribulation, that we may be able to comfort them which are in any trouble, by the comfort wherewith we ourselves are comforted of God (II Corinthians 1:3–4).*

Discretion and Potiphar's Wife

The trouble began in the heart of Potiphar's wife. It has been said that at the heart of every problem is a problem of the heart. *The heart is deceitful above all things, and desperately wicked: who can know it* (Jeremiah 17:9)? Discretion knows not to follow her heart; the foolish follow their feelings and their own will. For example, lust of the flesh, lust of the eyes, and the pride of life were in the heart of Potiphar's wife. She was of the world. *For all that is in the world, the lust of the flesh, and the lust of the eyes, and the pride of life, is not of the Father, but is of the world* (I John 2:16). Potiphar's wife, a married woman, wanted Joseph, the overseer in their house. Joseph was there because he had been sold by his brothers in Canaan to merchants going to Egypt.

> *And Joseph was brought down to Egypt; and Potiphar, an officer of Pharaoh, captain of the guard, an Egyptian, bought him of the hands of the Ishmaelites, which had brought him down thither. And the LORD was with Joseph, and he was a prosperous man; and he was in the house of his master the Egyptian. And his master saw*

*that the LORD was with him, and that the
LORD made all that he did to prosper in
his hand. [...] And he left all that he had
in Joseph's hand; and he knew not ought
he had, save the bread which he did eat.
And Joseph was a goodly person, and well
favoured. And it came to pass after these
things, that his master's wife cast her eyes
upon Joseph; and she said, Lie with me
(Genesis 39:1–3,6–7).*

Potiphar's wife *cast her eyes upon Joseph.* She was
looking for a man other than her husband. Flattery
would have been one of her tactics to lure Joseph
into her net. *A man that flattereth his neighbour
spreadeth a net for his feet* (Proverbs 29:5). Why does
a hunter spread out a net? He wants to catch prey.

The adulteress also wants to catch prey; she spreads
the net by appealing to a man's Pride with flattering
words. Potiphar's wife would have said something
like, "You're so strong, so handsome, and so wise."
Her intention was clear. She said, *"Lie with me."*

Our trouble began at the local mall. For six years we
rented a kiosk at the mall and sold gourmet coffees

and teas. My husband was normally there Monday through Friday, and I took over on Saturdays. We closed the kiosk on Sundays. Our motto at the kiosk was "Coffee, Conversation, and Mall Information." The mall has been described as a small, sleepy mall, which is true. There was plenty of time to talk to customers and those who walked the mall for exercise.

We were allowed to put out free gospel tracts, John and Roman booklets, and Bibles, so it was also a place of ministry. There were even some people who prayed to receive Christ right at the kiosk! One Thursday, a woman came to the kiosk to buy a cup of coffee. Driver's wife (not her real name) began coming every Thursday for coffee and conversation with my husband.

A couple weeks later my husband came home with a binder full of information about supplements that she had given him to copy. He was seeing three specialists at the time for health problems and was eager to find something that would help. I looked through the binder and just found the ordinary assortment of supplements.

The next Thursday, I went to the mall to pick up my husband, and Driver's wife was at the kiosk. My husband introduced me, and then I handed her the binder. I thanked her, but, after looking through it, found nothing that would help my husband's health problems. Driver's wife glared at me. Suddenly, she changed her angry look to a sad expression. She said how she liked talking to my husband because her husband was so mean and so much older than she was. "Your husband is so kind, so caring, and he listens to me," she said with a smile.

That was a red flag. Any woman who complains about her own husband and has only flattering words for another woman's husband is trouble. Discretion kept my husband from being drawn away by flattery. *Discretion shall preserve thee, understanding shall keep thee. [...] To deliver thee from the strange woman, even from the stranger which flattereth with her words* (Proverbs 2:11,16). Discretion[35] in this verse comes from the Hebrew word *mezimmah* (mez-im-maw') "meaning a plan, usually evil, sometimes good [sagacity]." In Proverbs 2:11, it would mean "sagacity; keenness in judgment; discernment." It is sensing trouble.

The next Sunday, Driver's wife came to our church. She came to every service. She cast her eyes on my husband and looked for every opportunity to stand very close to him and talk. The flatterer was spreading her net. It was noticeable. A lady from church eventually confronted my husband about Driver's wife. When she mentioned the wife's name, my husband replied, "Oh, her," in that tone of voice that clearly indicated his annoyance. The lady was relieved and told my husband she thought that my husband was chasing Driver's wife. He made sure she didn't stand right next to him anymore and avoided her as much as possible. *Abstain from all appearance of evil* (I Thessalonians 5:22).

Meanwhile, an odd thing started happening. A few ladies in the church, who had been friendly to me, started being cold and avoided talking to me. I began observing that Driver's wife would sit by one woman for several weeks, then sit with another for several weeks, and the pattern continued. Each of those women stopped being friendly to me. Why? One Sunday morning, I finally asked God to show me the reason. That very morning God told me.

The woman who taught the opening children's Sunday school lesson had chosen Philippians 2:3 which says, *Let nothing be done through strife or vainglory; but in lowliness of mind let each esteem other better than themselves.* While studying that verse, she found out that the word *strife*[36] has a different meaning than we normally use the word. It is translated from the Greek word *eritheia* (e-ree-thay'-a), a political term denoting "a self-seeking pursuit of political office by unfair means." It's someone using deceit to gain favor and followers. The word *strife*[37] in Philippians 2:3 also refers to "a spinner, weaver, a worker in wool." *Strife,* in this verse, actually means, "Pulling the wool over their eyes." God was telling me that Driver's wife was lying about me to those ladies to get them to side with her.

I had been feeling down because I had to face another Sunday of the "cold friendlies," but God uplifted me with that lesson. He answered my prayer. He knew what was happening, and no matter who Driver's wife won over by deceit, God was on the side of truth, the side I had chosen to be on. Psalm 119:30 states, *I have chosen the way of truth: thy judgments have I laid before me,* which perfectly expressed it.

God's judgments are righteous, just as Psalm 19:9 says, *The fear of the LORD is clean, enduring for ever: the judgments of the LORD are true and righteous altogether."* This verse is the foundation of Discretion—judgments that are true and righteous.

During that time, we received a call from our friend Patrick. He had been at work, minding his own business, when a newly-hired female worker came into the room and squeezed his behind. He turned around and told her that was very inappropriate behavior, especially at the place where they worked. It was a community help organization. She fled. No one else was in the room. The next thing he knew, the social worker on staff called him into the office and accused him of sexual harassment. This sounds like Joseph's story.

There were no witnesses to defend Patrick and, being a man, of course, he must be guilty; the female worker was so upset. What made it worse was that his boss of many years also believed the lie. Patrick transferred to a different department, cut his hours, and called us to pray that he would find another job quickly. He did what he could to avoid the woman until he could leave. Within a few weeks, God opened up a maintenance job that offered better pay and benefits including paid vacation. We all praised God for answered prayer. By the way, Patrick called after that and said he'd received a dollar-an-hour raise.

Discretion is not fooled by crying or a woman who is upset. Since there were no witnesses, it was a case of her word against his. Someone's story is a lie. King Solomon had to deal with two women who claimed the same baby as her own. Obviously, one of them was lying. Using God-given wisdom, Solomon knew the real mother would not want her baby hurt, even if it meant giving him up.

> Then said the king, The one saith, This is my son that liveth, and thy son is the dead: and the other saith, Nay; but thy son is the dead, and my son is the living. And the king said, Bring me a sword. And they brought a sword before the king. And the king said, Divide the living child in two, and give half to the one, and half to the other. Then spake the woman whose the living child was unto the king, for her bowels yearned upon her son, and she said,

O my lord, give her the living child, and in no wise slay it. But the other said, Let it be neither mine nor thine, but divide it. Then the king answered and said, Give her the living child, and in no wise slay it; she is the mother thereof (I Kings 3:23–27).

Discretion understands how to reveal the truth. She is like an honest judge in a court case, determined to administer justice and judgment.

Joseph confronted Potiphar's wife with truth to try and stop her advances. *There is none greater in this house than I; neither hath he kept back any thing from me but thee, because thou art his wife: how then can I do this great wickedness, and sin against God* (Genesis 39:9)? Joseph knew that fornication is great wickedness; it is sinning against God. The confrontation didn't deter Potiphar's wife. Joseph had to endure her temptations day after day. We read this in Genesis 39:10 *And it came to pass, as she spake to Joseph day by day, that he hearkened not unto her, to lie by her, or be with her.*

Driver's wife didn't give up either. She was determined to get my husband alone with her. Knowing he wanted relief from his health problems, she told him about a health professional who supposedly would be able to help him. She said that she would have to introduce him, so she would take him in her car. My husband knew that would be very wrong and asked for the professional's phone number. She refused. Finally, at church one Sunday morning, my husband insisted that she give him the phone number. A visitor and I were listening, so she reluctantly wrote down a phone number but no name. When he got home, he decided that the whole thing sounded suspicious and threw the number away.

Discretion keeps us safe from the one who flatters herself by thinking "I'm the one who knows what's needed." "I'm the one who really cares." The flatterer deceives herself as well as others. Beware, and remember the snare.

Driver's wife's next move was very bold. We arrived early for Wednesday evening Bible study and, as usual, I sat in the pew first, and my husband sat by the aisle. Driver's wife came in, slowed down as she passed us, and in a very sexy voice said, "Hi, Tony." She then walked to a pew down front. I couldn't believe it; she was openly flirting with my husband in front of me and in church. No one else heard her, so there were no witnesses or evidence to reveal the truth. When we got home, my husband reassured me that he would put a stop to it all.

The next day was Thursday, and, true to his word, as soon as Driver's wife came to the kiosk, my husband told her that she was never to buy coffee from him again and to "stop getting between my wife and me." She ran off crying. When my husband got home, he told me what had happened and decided he should tell our pastor. It was good judgment. Driver's wife had already called Pastor and cried that my husband had told her not to come to church anymore. She lied. My husband hadn't said anything about church. He told Pastor what had really happened and why.

Like many pastors, he dealt with the matter from the pulpit. He preached on lying, gossiping, and flirting. He gave a great lesson on the word *lasciviousness* found in Galatians 5:19–21:

> *Now the works of the flesh are manifest, which are these; Adultery, fornication, uncleanness, lasciviouness, Idolatry,*

witchcraft, hatred, variance, emulations, wrath, strife, seditions, heresies, Envyings, murders, drunkenness, revellings, and such like: of the which I tell you before, as I have also told you in time past, that they which do such things shall not inherit the kingdom of God.

The word *lasciviousness*[38] (la-siv'-i-us-nes) is from the Greek feminine noun *aselgeia* (a-se'l-gay-a) meaning "unbridled lust, excess, licentiousness, wantonness, outrageousness, shamelessness, insolence." It is lust of the flesh without any restraints. In our flesh we cannot have victory over lust of the flesh or even want victory, but through the presence and power of the Holy Spirit in us, we can conquer. *And they that are Christ's have crucified the flesh with the affections and lusts. If we live in the Spirit, let us also walk in the Spirit* (Galatians 5:24–25).

About two weeks after my husband had confronted Driver's wife, God woke me up out of a sound sleep at four o'clock in the morning with the definite command, "Go see Driver, her husband." When my husband got up, we talked about it. He said we should wait two weeks and use that time to pray for his salvation. Why else would God want us to visit him? We waited and prayed, and then on a Wednesday evening when we knew Driver's wife should have left for Bible study, we went to Driver's house.

Driver's wife had told us her husband was "so mean and so much older than she was." When we got to their home, it certainly didn't look like she had a mean husband. The porch was loaded with knick-knack decorations obviously chosen by a woman. For a "mean" husband, he let her decorate the way she wanted. We heard dogs barking, then Driver came around the corner of the barn. We were stunned. He wasn't "so much older" at all. He happened to be only two years older. He was friendly enough until my husband introduced us. "Hi, I am Anthony, and this is my wife, Nancy." Suddenly his body language changed.

His arms folded, eyes narrowed, and his expression became angry. Why would he react that way to hearing our names? We hadn't met him before. No one at church had ever visited or spoken to him. The only person who could have been talking to him about us was his wife, and it wasn't complimentary.

Both my husband and I realized he wouldn't be open to the gospel, so my husband wisely made our visit brief and simply invited him to church. He said he had his own church. This was why God had us come? I decided to tell Driver the truth. I told him how God woke me up with the clear command to come see him.

"Is there something we can pray with you about or a question we could answer? I'm not understanding why God wanted us to come," I said.

In an angry tone, he replied, "All I want from you is to stop getting between my wife and me." Those were the exact words that my husband had said to his wife! No wonder he was angry.

Potiphar reacted the same way when his wife lied to him about Joseph.

> *And she spake unto him according to these words, saying, The Hebrew servant, which thou hast brought unto us, came in unto me to mock me: And it came to pass, as I lifted up my voice and cried, that he left his garment with me, and fled out. And it*

came to pass, when his master heard the words of his wife, which she spake unto him, saying, After this manner did thy servant to me; that his wrath was kindled (Genesis 39:17–19).

Potiphar put Joseph in prison.

My husband was not arrested, but tragically, there are innocent men and woman who have been falsely accused and have been arrested. Lying is a terrible sin. Revelation 21:7–8 tells us God's judgment on all liars:

He that overcometh shall inherit all things; and I will be his God, and he shall be my son. But the fearful, and unbelieving, and the abominable, and murderers, and whoremongers, and sorcerers, and idolaters, and all liars, shall have their part in the lake which burneth with fire and brimstone: which is the second death.

Now there was another problem. I was angry. I cried all the way to Wednesday evening Bible study. I cried for a husband who defended a wife who lied about him, lied to him, and flirted behind his back. I cried for his soul. He was so angry that he didn't even want to hear the gospel. I was angry at people at church who believed her lies. Was there no wisdom?

Then God sent Penny. On the very evening I was too upset to reason through the situation, Penny came out to the church parking lot to say hello after Bible study. Penny and I have shared a lot over the years. She wanted to know why I was so upset. I told her. She said she would pray that the truth be known about Driver's wife. I knew God had sent her, because He didn't want me to leave the church. I was going to leave. Instead, He was giving me this lesson on Discretion. I have stayed and seen the answer to my prayers. The answer will be in the next pillars, Counsel and Reproof.

May Discretion guide you to truth and righteous judgment.

Further Study for Discretion

Author's Note: The word *discretion* is not capitalized below because the definitions are different than the meaning for the pillar of Discretion.

The word *discretion*[39] is also translated from the Hebrew word *ta'am* (tah'-am) meaning "a taste; perception, by implication intelligence; reason, understanding, judgment." The only verse with this meaning for discretion is Proverbs 11:22, *As a jewel of gold in a swine's snout, so is a fair woman which is without discretion.*

1. What is Proverbs 11:22 teaching about this meaning for discretion?

2. Proverbs 19:11 states, *The discretion of a man deferreth his anger; and it is his glory to pass over a transgression.* This is the only verse that *discretion*[40] comes from the Hebrew word *sekel* (seh'-kel), meaning "intelligence, by implication success: knowledge, policy, sense, wisdom, prudence." The word *deferreth*[41] is only found in this verse and means "draw out, lengthen, prolong, outlive."

3. What is Proverbs 19:11 teaching about this meaning for discretion?

The other word translated to *discretion*[42] is *towbunah* (to-boo-naw'), meaning "intelligence, by implication an argument; by extension caprice (whim, impulse, escapade): reason, skillfulness, wisdom." Obviously, *towbunah* has good and bad meanings. In Scripture, it is only used in Jeremiah 10:12: *He hath made the earth by his power, he hath established the world by his wisdom, and hath stretched out the heavens by his discretion.*

4. What does Jeremiah 10:12 say about God and discretion?

Pillar #6

Counsel

Hear counsel, and receive instruction, that thou mayest be wise in thy latter end (Proverbs 19:20).

When I graduated from college with a B.A. degree in psychology, I discovered something: Professional counselors were not in high demand. In fact, those with a master's degree or doctorate were applying for positions that only required a bachelor's degree. I had a loan to repay and monthly bills, so I ended up working for a while as kitchen staff in a nursing home located in a Jewish community. I never did pursue a career in counseling. I did find Someone far above Sigmund Freud, B.F. Skinner, and John Watson to teach me about Counsel. Isaiah 9:6 declares who He is, *For unto us a child is born, unto us a son is given: and the government shall be upon his shoulder: and his name shall be called Wonderful, Counsellor, The mighty God, The everlasting Father, The Prince of Peace.*

As Creator of the body, soul, and spirit, the Counselor knows all about us. He knows our thoughts, our feelings, our strengths, and weaknesses. Counsel is His to give. *Counsel is mine, and sound wisdom: I am understanding; I have strength* (Proverbs 8:14).

There was a king of Judah, Hezekiah, who was dying. He talked to God about it, which was a wise thing to do.

> *I beseech thee, O LORD, remember now how I have walked before thee in truth and with a perfect heart, and have done that which is good in thy sight. And Hezekiah wept sore (II Kings 20:3).*

Remember that Jesus wept? He is called a man of sorrows in Isaiah 53:3. In Romans 12:15 God commands, *Rejoice with them that do rejoice, and weep with them that weep.* God weeps with us in time of sorrow. He also comforts. For Hezekiah, comfort came in a message from the prophet Isaiah.

> *Thus saith the LORD, the God of David thy father, I have heard thy prayer, I have seen thy tears: behold, I will heal thee: on the third day thou shalt go up unto the house of the LORD. And I will add unto thy days fifteen years; and I will deliver thee and this city out of the hand of the king of Assyria; and I will defend this city for mine own sake, and for my servant David's sake. And Isaiah said, Take a lump of figs. And they took and laid it on the boil, and he recovered (II Kings 20:5b–7).*

I've never seen fig ointment with the antibiotic creams, yet it worked for Hezekiah because the Lord, the Great Physician, prescribed it.

Another king of Judah, Asa, had diseased feet. By the way, the name Asa means "physician."

> *And Asa in the thirty and ninth year of his reign was diseased in his feet, until his disease was exceeding great: yet in his*

disease he sought not the LORD, but to the physicians. And Asa slept with his fathers, and died in the one and fortieth year of his reign (II Chronicles 16:12–13).

The physicians he sought would have been magicians or soothsayers. He suffered for two years but refused to pray to the Lord.

The question is: Are we crying out to God like Hezekiah or ignoring Him like Asa?

Seek the LORD

Seek the LORD as the Great Physician. We need doctors, nurses, chiropractors, dieticians, and other people trained to help us physically, yet we should seek the LORD. Ask Him to give the surgeon wisdom and to guide his hands. Pray for a right diagnosis. Beseech Him for a sale on figs. Seriously, the Great Physician knows who we need to see and what treatment we may need. Paul traveled with Luke, the beloved physician, as a companion. The LORD is not against medical help.

Yes, at times, God does heal miraculously without treatments. The following true story is an example. Bill Revello had diabetes as well as other medical problems. His wife had prayed over and over again that he would not need his foot amputated because of poor circulation and infection, which had already required two toes on that foot to be removed. Finally, the day came when the surgeon said that his foot had to be amputated or infection would kill him. His foot was black, very painful, and very swollen. Bill agreed to the amputation. The morning of his scheduled surgery, his wife sent me this text:

> *No surgery!!!!!! Bill has literally revived. The skin looks totally normal. His pain is so down and his leg is not hurting as much and the swelling in the foot is down two inches. Surgeon said, let's wait, he can always come back and the surgeon would start with just taking the big toe. God is good and so merciful. He has given us a gift. Still need prayer for healing, but this is a miracle.*[43]

What an answer to prayer! I had never heard of an amputation being cancelled on the very day it was scheduled because it wasn't needed. Bill went home to the Lord recently and never did have his foot amputated.

At times, God does not heal as we so desire. We still need to seek the LORD as Comforter and Lord of peace. When my dad died, God gave me wonderful peace. *And the peace of God, which passeth all understanding, shall keep your hearts and minds through Christ Jesus* (Philippians 4:7). Think about that verse. The word *keep*[44] is from the Greek word *phroureo* (froo-reh'-o) meaning "to mount guard as a sentinel, protect." The peace of God protects our hearts and minds from sinful, crazy thoughts. There are people today sitting in insane asylums because they refused to seek the LORD when tragedy struck. God does not intend sorrow and suffering to lead us to a padded room (delightful as that may sound) but to Himself, our refuge. A thought that kept me going in college after a broken engagement was this: When we come to the place where there is nothing left but God, God is enough. He really is all we need.

Seek the LORD as your heavenly Father for daily needs. When the disciples had asked Jesus to teach them to pray, Jesus included in the pattern for prayer these words, *Give us this day our daily bread* (Matthew 6:11). Our family has seen God provide groceries, clothes, vehicles, and money for bills. When I prayed for potatoes (it's the Irish in me), God gave us a grocery sack of potatoes. When the sack was gone, God gave us a fifty-pound bag of potatoes. I needed casual shoes years ago and found a brand-new pair of name brand (normally $100) shoes at a consignment shop for only $10. They fit perfectly, were comfortable, and lasted for years. That's God's blessing. We've had cars given to us. Unexpected checks, extra work, and excused bills have been the means God has used to care for us through the years. The LORD as a loving Father meets needs.

Seek the LORD as Counselor when making decisions. In I Samuel 30, we read about David and his men coming home to Ziklag. The Amalekites had burned the city and taken their wives, sons, and daughters captive. Out of grief and distress, the people talked of stoning David; out of grief and distress, David sought the LORD. *And David enquired*

at the LORD, saying, Shall I pursue after this troop?
shall I overtake them? And he answered him, Pursue:
for thou shalt surely overtake them, and without fail
recover all (I Samuel 30:8). It would have been easy
to succumb to feelings instead of asking for God's
Counsel, but feelings will lead us astray. Stoning
David would not have rescued their loved ones.

Years ago, my husband and I had an important decision to make. The following is an excerpt from the
letter my husband sent to friends:

> *More than four years have passed since I*
> *resigned as pastor of Bible Baptist Church*
> *in Missouri. During that time, I have had*
> *the opportunity to preach in ten different*
> *churches. The wait for the right church has*
> *been discouraging at times. On a Sunday*
> *evening this past June, Nancy and I sat in*
> *church wondering if God wanted us to go*
> *into full-time ministry again or just stay*
> *here in Keokuk. While our pastor preached,*
> *we asked God to speak to our hearts about*
> *what we should do. A couple minutes later*
> *our pastor emphatically stated, "Go for-*
> *ward! The Lord said, Go forward!" Our*

*hearts leaped with hope and joy. God had
spoken. We are to go! Since then we have
been preparing to move.*

We did move later that year to start a church in
Wisconsin whose state motto happens to be
"Forward."

Seek the LORD as Judge. When the children of
Israel were in the wilderness, an incident happened that required God's judgment. The son of
an Israelite mother and an Egyptian father strove in
the camp with a man of Israel. The son blasphemed
the name of God and cursed. *And they put him in
ward, that the mind of the LORD might be shewed
them* (Leviticus 24:12). This is wisdom: seeking the
mind of the LORD. Those who heard him blas-
pheme and curse may have had their own ideas
about the penalty for such a sin, yet they sought the
LORD. The son was guilty, and the Judge sentenced
him to death by stoning. This established a statute
given in Leviticus 24:16, *And he that blasphemeth
the name of the LORD, he shall surely be put to
death, and all the congregation shall certainly stone
him: as well the stranger, as he that is born in the
land, when he blasphemeth the name of the LORD,*

shall be put to death. The Lord has the authority to declare what should be done about a matter. He sees the end from the beginning and knows the impact of sin and its judgment. Our part is to agree with God's Word.

Agree with God's Word

God's Counsel never contradicts God's Word. There is a tendency to have our own ideas about solving problems apart from God's Word. Consider Naaman the Syrian. He had position and power but was plagued with the fatal disease of leprosy. *Now Naaman, captain of the host of the king of Syria, was a great man with his master, and honourable, because by him the LORD had given deliverance unto Syria: he was also a mighty man in valour, but he was a leper* (II Kings 5:1). Hope was kindled when his wife's little Hebrew servant girl said that the prophet in Samaria, Elisha, could cure his leprosy. When Naaman arrived at Elisha's house, he did not get the cure he was expecting. Elisha himself didn't even come to the door. *And Elisha sent a messenger unto him, saying, Go and wash in Jordan seven times, and thy flesh shall come again to thee, and thou shalt be clean. But Naaman was wroth, and went away, and said, Behold, I thought, He will surely come out to me, and stand, and call on the name of the LORD his God, and strike his hand over the place, and recover the leper. Are not Abana and Pharpar, rivers of Damascus, better than all the waters of Israel? may I not wash in them, and be clean? So he turned and went away in a rage* (II Kings 5:10–12). We can do the same thing by searching in God's Word for what we want to find that agrees with us. If we don't like what it says, we turn away from God's Counsel. We may even convince ourselves that we are the exception; therefore, we ought to have our way. Naaman would have died of leprosy, but his servants intervened. They helped him agree that God's Counsel was better than his ideas. *And his servants came near, and spake unto him, and said, My father, if the prophet had bid thee do some great thing, wouldest thou not have done it? how much rather then, when he saith to thee, Wash, and be clean? Then went he down, and dipped himself seven times in Jordan, according to the saying of the man of God: and his flesh came again like unto the flesh of a little child, and he was clean* (II Kings 5:13–15). Naaman, his servants, and his family were so glad that Naaman obeyed the Counsel of the prophet. Following God's Counsel is always best.

Tragically, many people turn to humanistic psychology for answers to life's problems instead of God's Word. For example, talking solves all problems is the wisdom of man. Peace talks will bring peace, right? Obviously, talking hasn't worked. Why not? The reason is that this philosophy is from humanistic psychology: the idea that man, not God, is the central focal point. The counsel of humanistic psychologists is that we must find self-worth, self-efficacy, and self-actualization. Self-worth focuses us on ourselves not God. It's believing, "I am worthy." Interestingly, the words *worth*[45] and *worship* both come from the Old English word *weorth* meaning "worth, value." In Christ, our value is not in who we are but whose we are, children of the Lord of glory. He is worthy. *Thou art worthy, O Lord, to receive glory and honour and power: for thou hast created all things, and for thy pleasure they are and were created* (Revelation 4:11). Self-efficacy is the concept that man has the power to produce effects and to solve all problems. For example, in 1912, man thought he had designed an unsinkable ship. Captain Edward Smith is quoted as saying, "God Himself could not sink this ship!"[46] In the middle of the night, on its maiden voyage, the Titanic, hit an iceberg and sank. Investigation of the tragedy revealed that overconfidence and carelessness cost the lives of over fifteen hundred people. Man cannot solve all problems because he really doesn't know what's ahead. God knows. *He* [God] *revealeth the deep and secret things: he knoweth what is in the darkness, and the light dwelleth with him* (Daniel 2:22). Self-actualization is the idea that man needs to "find himself." The foundation is that man is inherently good and just needs the right influences to bring out the good. Remember Judas Iscariot? He was in the very presence of Jesus Himself, the best influence of all, yet he remained a thief. The apostle Paul knew that man is not inherently good. *For I know that in me (that is, in my flesh,) dwelleth no good thing: for to will is present with me; but how to perform that which is good I find not* (Romans 7:18). Counsel based on humanistic psychology is in direct opposition to God's Word. We should seek Counsel that focuses us on God not self.

When I realized Driver's wife had cast her eyes on my husband, I sought Counsel from godly ladies who had been involved in ministry for more than forty years. They know God's Word, and they know me. I could trust them to tell me the truth. All three agreed that avoiding Driver's wife and not talking to her or about her was the right course of action. *He that goeth about as a talebearer revealeth secrets: therefore meddle not with him that flattereth with his lips* (Proverbs 20:19). It has been a great lesson in temperance or self-control. In the flesh, we want to tell all we know about a matter. In the Spirit, we can refrain our tongue and be quiet. God also showed me in His Word to be on guard as the devil will attack even at church. *Put on the whole armour of God, that ye may be able to stand against the wiles of the devil* (Ephesians 6:11). The armour of God would be a study by itself, so I'll just say that God expects us to be ready when the attack comes. When in need of Counsel, we must be sure that Counsel agrees with God's Word.

Trust in the LORD

God's Counsel is to trust Him. Trust in the LORD relieves us of anger, anxiety, and anguish. When we believe God's promises, we can cease from anger. *Cease from anger, and forsake wrath: fret not thyself in any wise to do evil* (Psalm 37:8). Visiting Driver was God's way of exposing more of the problem with Driver's wife. Talking to Penny helped as well, but thoughts of revenge on Driver's wife kept plaguing me. Exactly two weeks later, during my morning devotions, I poured out my heart to the LORD as Psalm 62:7–8 tells us to do. *In God is my salvation and my glory: the rock of my strength, and my refuge, is in God. Trust in him at all times; ye people, pour out your heart before him: God is a refuge for us. Selah* (Psalm 62:7–8).

I read Scripture while I pray. That morning I told my heavenly Father that I was tired of feeling angry and asked that He take the anger away. I had been reading the book of Romans, and, after that prayer to God, He spoke to me through Romans 12:19 *Dearly beloved,* I stopped reading. God was calling me "Dearly beloved!" I was overcome with the thought. I resumed reading. *Avenge not yourselves, but rather give place unto wrath: for it is written, Vengeance is mine; I will repay, saith the Lord.* My anger drained away. God Himself would take vengeance. I was at peace again resting in His promise. *Say not thou, I will recompense evil; but wait on the LORD, and he shall save thee* (Proverbs 20:22).

God's Counsel also relieves anxiety. When anxious thoughts trouble us and fears overwhelm us, we are prone to get desperate. We will listen to anyone and do anything. Life becomes a frenzied search. "There must be something to help me. I must find it. I can't take this anymore!"

A snowstorm had begun as my husband and I were on our way home from a cleaning job one night. I was driving and slowed from 45 mph to 35 mph as the snow covered the state highway; visibility was very poor. We were still about thirty-five miles from home when panic began to overwhelm me. I thought "I can't do this. I just can't keep driving in this whiteout. God, please help me." Suddenly a semi-truck and trailer passed us and moved into the lane in front of us. He drove out of sight in the swirling snowfall but left visible tire tracks. God answered my prayer. We followed the tracks all the way to the exit, and I kept repeating Isaiah 41:10 *Fear thou not; for I am with thee: be not dismayed; for I am thy God: I will strengthen thee; yea, I will help thee; yea, I will uphold thee with the right hand of my righteousness.* God's promises are trustworthy and will calm the anxious soul.

When in anguish, weighed down by sorrow, trust in the LORD. For example, Ruth, the Moabitess, was a young widow who followed her widowed Jewish mother-in-law, Naomi, from Moab to Bethlehem. Ruth and Naomi were grieving the death of loved ones. They were very poor. Ruth was a Gentile among Jews, a stranger. Her future looked bleak; however, Ruth found a refuge in the LORD. When a landowner named Boaz met her gleaning in his field, she wanted to know why she found grace in his eyes. *And Boaz answered and said unto her, It hath fully been shewed me, all that thou hast done unto thy mother in law since the death of thine husband: and how thou hast left thy father and thy mother, and the land of thy nativity, and art come unto a people which thou knewest not heretofore. The LORD recompense thy work, and a full reward be given thee of the LORD God of Israel, under whose wings thou art come to trust* ((Ruth 2:11–12). Her trust in the LORD made Ruth willing to care for her mother-in-law despite her own sorrow. God blessed that trust. Ruth and Boaz married, and years later, their great grandson, David, wrote about trust. *Hear my cry, O God; attend unto my prayer. From the end of the earth will I cry unto thee, when my heart is overwhelmed: lead me to the rock that is higher than I. For thou hast been a shelter for me, and a strong tower from the enemy. I will abide in thy tabernacle for ever: I will trust in the covert of thy wings. Selah* (Psalm 61:1–4).

When we lived in Keokuk, Iowa, we studied eagles. Every winter, hundreds of bald eagles came down from the North to fish in the Mississippi River. A dam for the power plant had been built across the river, which kept the water from freezing over. Watching the eagles fly and swoop down to catch fish was a tremendous sight. Since we were observing bald eagles, we borrowed library books to learn more about them. One author wrote that no one knows why the eagle puts a prickly pine branch into the nest. God knows, and He let us know. *As an eagle stirreth up her nest, fluttereth over her young, spreadeth abroad her wings, taketh them, beareth them on her wings: So the LORD alone did lead him, and there was no strange god with him* (Deuteronomy 32:11–12). The eagle uses the prickly pine branch when it's time to stir up her nest. The young eagle gets poked and poked until it gets up and climbs onto its mother's wings. The young eagle is carried away from the comfortable nest to the heights.

God is poking some of us. Affliction is like the prickly pine branch. *It is good for me that I have been afflicted; that I might learn thy statutes* (Psalm 119:71). Physical struggles, emotional pain, and financial problems are meant for our good. God is teaching us to trust Him and to lean on His strength.

> *Hast thou not known? hast thou not heard, that the everlasting God, the LORD, the Creator of the ends of the earth, fainteth not, neither is weary? there is no searching of his understanding. He giveth power to the faint; and to them that have no might he increaseth strength. Even the youths shall faint and be weary, and the young men shall utterly fall: But they that wait upon the LORD shall renew their strength; they shall mount up with wings as eagles; they shall run, and not be weary; and they shall walk, and not faint (Isaiah 40:28–31).*

When the pine branch of affliction has done its work, the LORD will lift us up to heights previously unknown. He will help us *"mount up with wings as eagles."* We will have greater Understanding and the joy of being nearer to God. Let the sight of an eagle in flight be a reminder to Trust in the LORD.

After we seek the LORD, agree with God's Word, and trust in the LORD, we will be rewarded. We will receive God's promise.

Receive His Promise

God's Counsel cannot be defeated. *There is no wisdom nor understanding nor counsel against the LORD* (Proverbs 21:30). We may have to wait, but God will perform what He promises. A man named Simeon, who lived in Jerusalem, was given a specific promise from God. *And it was revealed unto him by the Holy Ghost, that he should not see death, before he had seen the Lord's Christ* (Luke 2:26). Thousands of years had passed since God promised the Messiah in Genesis 3:15, but Simeon had faith that God would let him see the Saviour before he died. We don't know when he was given this promise or how much time passed, but we do know that God fulfilled His promise to Simeon. When everyone was to be taxed by order of Caesar Augustus, Simeon was moved by the Holy Spirit to go to the temple. *And he came by the Spirit into the temple: and when the parents brought in the child Jesus, to do for him after the custom of the law, Then took he him up in his arms, and blessed God, and said, Lord, now lettest thou thy servant depart in peace, according to thy word: For mine eyes have seen thy salvation, Which thou hast prepared before the face of all people; A light to lighten the Gentiles, and the glory of thy people Israel* (Luke 2:27–32). Simeon believed and received God's promise.

God promised me that He would avenge me of my adversary, so I waited. Meanwhile, Driver's wife changed her tactics. She tried a feigned apology to regain favor with my husband. On a Sunday morning when the pastor was absent, she feigned an apology by saying, "If I have hurt you, I'm sorry. I didn't mean to hurt you."

That is not confession of sin. It's like saying to God, "If I have sinned, I'm sorry." If? What did you do? She had been raised Catholic and understood confession. I waited to see if she was genuinely sorry or if she was trying to deceive again. A few weeks later, she followed my husband out of church, looked both ways to be sure no one was around, got close, and again gushed, "Hi, Tony."

She hadn't changed at all; however, God was bringing about changes. At the end of the year, my husband decided to close down the coffee kiosk at the mall. Business had nearly come to a halt; it was time. Then a few months later during morning devotions, I reminded my heavenly Father of His promise to avenge me of my adversary. I did not ask in anger, but simply to acknowledge that I was waiting the fulfillment of His promise.

That evening, Driver's wife didn't come to Wednesday Bible study. She didn't come the next Sunday. After being absent for three weeks, the pastor announced that Driver's wife had told him that she had an eye problem. Her eyes were extremely dry, so she had to put in eyedrops every two hours and be in a particular position. Immediately, two thoughts came to mind. The first was that God had kept His promise to me, and the second was that God was very merciful to her. Her problem wasn't fatal or extremely painful. He was just in giving a woman who cast her eyes on another man an eye problem.

> *The Great, the Mighty God, the LORD of hosts, is his name, Great in counsel, and mighty in work: for thine eyes are open upon all the ways of the sons of men: to give every one according to his ways,*

and according to the fruit of his doings
(Jeremiah 32:18c–19).

Days, weeks, months, or even years may pass while we wait for God to fulfill His promises, but His promises never fail. He is the Mighty God.

When we need Counsel follow these steps:

1. Seek the LORD
2. Agree with God's Word
3. Trust in the LORD
4. Receive His Promise

Further Study for Counsel

Look up the verses then answer the questions.

1. According to Psalm 1:1, whose counsel is not to be followed?

Read I Kings 1:5–14.

2. Who decided to reign on his own?

3. Why did Nathan give Counsel to Bathsheba?

4. What Counsel did Nathan give?

Read II Samuel 20:13–22.

5. In what city did Sheba, son of Bichri, hide?

6. Who confronted Joab about the reason for the siege?

7. What was said in old time about the city of Abel?

8. What was the wise woman's Counsel?

9. According to Psalm 73:20–24, who shalt guide me with Counsel?

Pillar #7

Reproof

The ear that heareth the reproof of life abideth among the wise (Proverbs 15:31).

Reproof[47] is translated from the Hebrew word *towkachath* (toe-kakh-ath), meaning "correction, rebuke, reasoning." We normally think of Reproof in a negative sense, but to have wisdom, Reproof is necessary. How we respond to Reproof reveals if we are wise or not. Proverbs 17:10 says, *A reproof entereth more into a wise man than an hundred stripes into a fool.*

The steps of Reproof are confrontation, correction, and, if necessary, restitution.

Confrontation

"Excuse me, but you charged me the regular price instead of the sale price," said the customer to the salesclerk.

When the employee entered the supervisor's office, the supervisor said, "Your work record is not up to company standards, so we've decided to terminate your employment, effective immediately."

"Bruce, did you take my slippers?" Nancy asked her younger brother. "Yes," he replied with a laugh, "and I won't tell you where they are." "Mom! Bruce took my slippers and won't tell me where they are," Nancy yelled. (Sweet memories of my childhood.)

These are all examples of confrontation, the first step of Reproof. Notice that in each case there was something wrong—a mistake, unacceptable work performance, and being mischievous (pronounced *mis'-chi-vus*). Throughout our lives we have to confront others or be confronted ourselves because of accidental or intentional wrong.

The first confrontation recorded in God's Word is God asking Adam, *Hast thou eaten of the tree, whereof I commanded thee that thou shouldest not eat* (Genesis 3:11b)? God wanted Adam to admit that he had disobeyed God's command. God already knew that Adam had eaten the forbidden fruit, so the confrontation was not for knowledge but rather for confession. Adam's reply acknowledged his sin but also laid blame on his wife. *And the man said, The woman whom thou gavest to be with me, she gave me of the tree, and I did eat* (Genesis 3:12). Adam did not want to take full responsibility for his sin. Adam's descendants (that's us) have been blaming others for our own wrong decisions ever since that day in the Garden of Eden.

Some situations require immediate confrontation, such as being at the checkout and noticing that the store clerk didn't give you the sale price on an item or the self-checkout charged you the wrong price. The evidence is in front of you and the wrong can be resolved without delay.

Other situations require waiting for the facts or evidence before the confrontation. Remember Hiero and his gold laurel wreath crown? The wise will make sure of the facts. Facts may include getting two or more witnesses or other evidence to prove the truth especially when it's a matter involving a liar.

Driver's wife was such a situation. She had been absent from church for about two months when she suddenly returned. I thought the trial was over, but it wasn't. She didn't attend every service anymore and that helped. My husband and I were on guard, but knew another confrontation was inevitable. It would happen in front of the pastor and a deacon. If you are dealing with someone who just won't stop doing wrong, be ready to state facts instead of displaying feelings. Remember, Queen Esther had to restrain her feelings when she told the king of Haman's evil plot to kill the Jews. Because Driver's wife had gained favor with certain people and had gotten my husband in a case of her word against his, we had to wait on the Lord for just the right time to tell church leadership. When the day came to confront Driver's wife in front of the pastor and a deacon, we had the testimonies of two witnesses to verify that she was chasing my husband and telling lies about us. The result of the confrontation was that she agreed not to have any contact with my husband and not to talk about him or about me to anyone for any reason. She was warned that the consequences of breaking that promise would be serious.

It would be great to say that we never had trouble with her again, but sometimes it takes time to know if Reproof has been heeded or not. God instructs us to forgive all but not to trust all. *It is better to trust in the LORD than to put confidence in man* (Psalm 118:8). Forgiveness is freely given, but trust must be earned. Just saying that we will not lie, steal, flirt, be abusive, be drunk, or such like is worthless unless we prove it by our actions. The one being confronted may not admit the wrong or stop doing wrong, but at the right time confrontation is necessary. We cannot control how others react to confrontation, but through the Holy Spirit, we can forgive and pray for them.

Jesus used confrontation to bring conviction of sin. In John 8, the scribes and Pharisees brought a woman who had been caught in the act of adultery. They reminded Him of the law of Moses. *Now Moses in the law commanded us, that such should be stoned: but what sayest thou? This they said, tempting him, that they might have to accuse him.*

But Jesus stooped down, and with his finger wrote on the ground, as though he heard them not (John 8:5–6). Jesus already knew who had sinned by breaking His Law—all of them. He dealt first with the woman's accusers. *So when they continued asking him, he lifted up himself, and said unto them, He that is without sin among you, let him first cast a stone at her. And again he stooped down, and wrote on the ground* (John 8:7–8). Natural curiosity would have made the scribes and Pharisees look down to see what Jesus was writing. As His finger moved in the sand, it also moved in their hearts: Are you without sin? *And they which heard it, being convicted by their own conscience, went out one by one, beginning at the eldest, even unto the last: and Jesus was left alone, and the woman standing in the midst* (John 8:9). Adultery was condemned by Old Testament law; then, in the Sermon on the Mount, Jesus raised the standard for purity. The thought of committing adultery was as sinful as the act of adultery. *Ye have heard that it was said by them of old time, Thou shalt not commit adultery: But I say unto you, That whosoever looketh on a woman to lust after her hath committed adultery with her already in his heart* (Matthew 5:27–28). Conviction of sin silenced her accusers. After the scribes and Pharisees left, Jesus confronted the remaining sinner, the adulteress. She was still guilty and worthy of death. *When Jesus had lifted up himself, and saw none but the woman, he said unto her, Woman, where are those thine accusers? hath no man condemned thee? She said, No man, Lord. And Jesus said unto her, Neither do I condemn thee: go, and sin no more* (John 8:10–11). Jesus was not excusing her sin; instead, He was fulfilling the law of Moses. Deuteronomy 17:6 states, *At the mouth of two witnesses, or three witnesses, shall he that is worthy of death be put to death; but at the mouth of one witness he shall not be put to death.* Since Jesus was the only one left who knew her sin, He did not condemn her to death. The Law of Moses also condemned the adulterer to death according to Leviticus 20:10. Where was the adulterer? Jesus obviously understood that the woman's accusers were not really concerned about the Law of Moses being fulfilled. Jesus did uphold Old Testament Law and reprove the sinners. His Reproof was *"Go, and sin no more."*

Like the scribes and Pharisees, we may not have obvious sins to confess, but we may have sinful thoughts and secret sins. Like Jesus' handwriting on the ground, God's Word brings those sins to mind and convicts us. We may have obvious sins and need to heed to same message that the adulteress heard from Jesus, "*Go, and sin no more.*"

Correction

Reproof corrects us by commanding that we forsake sin. Just as Jesus told the adulteress to forsake her sin, Reproof would tell the thief to steal no more, the liar to stop lying, and the quick-tempered to control his anger. When we have heeded Reproof, the change in our lives will be evident.

Correction begins in childhood. Reproof is part of child rearing; wise fathers and mothers correct their children. Proverbs 29:15 states, *The rod and reproof give wisdom: but a child left to himself bringeth his mother to shame.* It's training children to do the right thing. "No, you have to finish your chores before you go out to play." "Yes, you must apologize for what you said." Wise children learn there are consequences for their words and actions.

As our heavenly Father, the LORD corrects us. *My son, despise not the chastening of the LORD; neither be weary of his correction: For whom the LORD loveth he correcteth; even as a father the son in whom he delighteth* (Proverbs 3:11–12). The LORD corrects out of love. He desires to remove the impurities in our lives as conforming us to His image pleases Him. What parent is not delighted in a wise, obedient child who chooses right instead of wrong?

When we disobey God's commands and teachings, He uses His Word to reprove us. *All scripture is given by inspiration of God, and is profitable for doctrine, for reproof, for correction, for instruction in righteousness: That the man of God may be perfect, thoroughly furnished unto all good works* (II Timothy 3:16–17).

We may have to correct a wrong involving someone else. If we have wronged anyone, we should apologize. The wrong may have been an accidental mistake or deliberate sin. Pride and Arrogancy fight hard against confessing wrongs and excuse them. "I'm sorry, but I was tired." "Well, I was wrong, but you made me angry. You even liked the dog food burgers I made you." An apology is simply confessing the wrong without excuses or claiming ignorance. "I'm sorry I lied. It was wrong. Will you forgive me?" Whether the one wronged forgives or not is not our responsibility. Our part is to ask forgiveness for specific sin. We must also ask God's forgiveness, since all sin is against God. He promises, *If we confess our sins, he is faithful and just to forgive us our sins, and to cleanse us from all unrighteousness* (I John 1:9).

Reproof alerts us to mistakes. Do we get defensive or acknowledge the error? Sometimes we may just need to laugh with everyone else. When I typed church bulletins years ago, sometimes there were typos despite proofreading. They were funny. Reproof reminds us that we are not perfect and it deflates our Pride. It also reminds us that others are not perfect either and will also make mistakes. A sign in my home reads: One nice thing about being imperfect is the joy it brings to others.

Not long ago, our children paid for airfare and a nine-day hotel stay for my husband and me to take a vacation in Arizona. Our plane arrived near midnight. We hired a taxi to our hotel in Glendale. Upon arrival, the young desk clerk told us that the computer system was being updated, so he couldn't look up our reservation. He assured us that he could find our room on the printout. He gave us a key to a room on the third floor. By that point it was about one o'clock in the morning. When we found the room, Anthony opened the door for me, and I started to walk in. Suddenly, he threw his arm in front of me and pushed me back out saying, "I'm sorry." The door shut.

"What's wrong?" I asked.

"Someone was in the bed!" he exclaimed.

We went back to the hotel clerk and handed him the room key. He was horrified. The look on his face said, "I just lost my job." He quickly looked up our reservation on the printout again, got a different key, and escorted us to a suite on the second floor. As the hotel clerk opened the door, I couldn't help calling out, "You hoo! Anybody home?" and began to laugh.

The clerk was amazed. "How can you laugh?"

"Are you kidding?" I replied. "This is the stuff movies are made of. This is funny."

By the way, we did lock the bolt lock every night of our stay. We wondered what the man in the room on the third floor thought when he sleepily saw his door closing. No more pepperoni pizza before bedtime!

Reproof challenges us to do better or do our best. When we make mistakes, we should learn from them. The following little poem I learned as a child expresses this thought:

> Good, better, best
> Never let it rest
> 'Til your good is better
> And your better—best.

The key is a humble, teachable spirit. For example, we will listen to the correction of a child.

"Mrs. Sari, your hair is a mess," Samantha commented as she entered Sunday school class.

I smiled. "I know, Samantha. Ever hear of a bad hair day?"

I did try to give my hair more attention after that. Even children know when something needs to be corrected.

We will listen to the feeble-minded, a demanding boss, a picky neighbor, or hubby.

"Honey, you're not wearing that are you?" Tom asked.

"What's wrong with this?" Maria wanted to know.

Tom said, "When you bend over it shows too much."

"Oh, I'll wear something else."

Maria did change and brought the dress to a friend who sewed. The friend lengthened the dress, added some accessories, and it was even prettier. Her husband was pleased and so was Maria.

Chastening is another means of correction. The word *chastening*[48] comes from the Hebrew word *muwcar* (moo-sawr') meaning "reproof, warning, or instruction; discipline, correction using words or blows." Some of God's children have tender hearts toward God, and chastening will be words. They hear a sermon, someone confronts them, or they read God's Word, and they are convicted of their wrong. They make things right. Some of God's children are *rashim kshim* (rah-sheem' k'-sheem), which is Hebrew for "hard heads." Ever hear someone say, "God took me to the woodshed"? (A woodshed was multifunctional. It was not only storage for firewood but was the place where the board of education was applied to the seat of learning.)

Now no chastening for the present seemeth to be joyous, but grievous: nevertheless afterward it yieldeth the peaceable fruit of righteousness unto them which are exercised thereby (Hebrews 12:11). That is the purpose of Reproof—to bring forth righteousness. To be right with God, we must correct our wrongs.

Jesus Christ says, *As many as I love, I rebuke and chasten: be zealous therefore, and repent* (Revelation 3:19). The word *repent*[49] in this verse comes from the Greek word *metanoeo* (met-an-o-eh'-o) meaning "to think differently; reconsider." We need to think about our ways. Do we have a zeal for God or are we casual about spiritual things? Reproof chastens us, so we will think differently about ourselves and agree with the Lord that we are in need of Him. The hymnwriter Annie S. Hawks expressed this thought in the hymn, *"I Need Thee Every Hour."*

When we heed Reproof, we abide among the wise. *He that walketh with wise men shall be wise: but a companion of fools shall be destroyed* (Proverbs 13:20). It's like the old saying: Birds of a feather flock together. Are we with the flock raiding the cornfield or singing with the flock on the telephone wire?

Correction is grievous unto him that forsaketh the way: and he that hateth reproof shall die (Proverbs 15:10). At twenty-two years old, Kevin lay in a casket. He had died in a car crash. At the funeral, my husband noticed Kevin's favorite rock song *"The Best of Both Worlds"* on display. This had become Kevin's philosophy. He had trusted Jesus as his Saviour as a boy and had been raised in the Knowledge of Jesus Christ. He wasn't a troublemaker. His family faithfully attended services at a Bible-believing church. As Kevin got into his late teen years, he believed the lie that he could love God and love the world. He spent more time with worldly friends, disregarding what he had learned from God's Word. His death proved that he couldn't have the best of both worlds. God commanded, *And thou shalt love the Lord thy God with all thy heart, and with all thy soul, and with all thy mind, and with all thy strength: this is the first commandment* (Mark 12:30). When we choose to follow the ways of the world, we no longer follow the Lord. Reproof may be death.

Whoso loveth instruction loveth knowledge: but he that hateth reproof is brutish (Proverbs 12:1). The word *brutish*[50] means "being consumed." The idea is one who is eaten up with such things as resentment, hatred, or rebellion. One response of the brutish to correction might be, "I'm just being me and doing my own thing; leave me alone." The attitude of the brutish toward Reproof is negative.

On the other hand, the attitude of the wise toward Reproof is positive. *A fool despiseth his father's instruction: but he that regardeth reproof is prudent* (Proverbs 15:5). If we think of Reproof as something beneficial, we will accept correction without getting angry or defensive. "Thank you for letting me know. I'll correct that." We understand that it truly is "for our own good."

Restitution

Reproof includes *restitution*[51] (res-ti-too'-shun) which means "the act of restoring; specifically, restoration of anything to its rightful owner; act of giving an equivalent for loss, damage, etc." The biblical principle of restitution is taught in Exodus 22:6 which states, *If fire break out, and catch in thorns, so that the stacks of corn, or the standing corn, or the field, be consumed therewith; he that kindleth the fire shall surely make restitution.* Whether the fire was an accident or not, whoever started the fire is to pay for the damages. The principle is clear. Did we damage something that belonged to someone else? We should pay for it.

Another biblical example of restitution is in the case of theft. Proverbs 6:30–31 says, *Men do not despise a thief, if he steal to satisfy his soul when he is hungry; But if he be found, he shall restore sevenfold; he shall give all the substance of his house.* Situation ethics teaches that we should excuse stealing for certain reasons like hunger. God's Word warns against all stealing even in the case of hunger. The thief was to pay back sevenfold; it was to teach the thief not to steal anymore. Remember the lesson on the Evil Way? Stealing is the Evil Way of satisfying needs. God's Way is asking for whatever we need. *Ask, and it shall be given you* (Matthew 7:7a). When we disobey this command and steal instead of asking, Reproof says to give back what was taken.

It was finally spring here in Central Wisconsin. Our daughter Rebecca and I were on the Saturday morning paper route enjoying the warmer weather. Then we saw it. On the front steps of a house on our route was a plate of Peanut Blossoms (those scrumptious peanut butter cookies with a chocolate kiss in the middle). The note read: Happy Spring! The Johnsons. How kind of them! It wasn't unusual for subscribers to give us something as their paper carriers. No one was around to thank, so we just took the cookies home. After eating them, we looked up the name and address on the paper route list to send a thank you note. The name of the family at that address was not the Johnsons. The Johnsons were neighbors that had left the plate of cookies for the folks on our route. We felt so embarrassed. We had stolen their cookies! A couple days later we showed up at the subscriber's door with another plate of homemade Peanut Blossoms and an apology. When the wife realized what had happened, she burst out laughing. The Johnsons had called and asked if they had enjoyed the cookies and were puzzled that they had disappeared. They thought maybe a dog had found them and dragged them off. We admitted that we were the dog and handed her the cookies. She thanked us and told our daughter that if she ever needed a reference, they would gladly give her one. After that, we were very careful to make sure that whatever was left at a house was clearly marked for the paper carrier before taking it.

When we make restitution as Reproof demands, our relationships will be better. We will replace or pay for whatever we tore, broke, marred, mowed down, accidently sold in the garage sale, or borrowed to a friend without the owner's permission. Someone may say, "Oh, that's okay. Forget it." Don't forget it; make it right. Several years ago, I gave my mother a small, tabletop storage cubicle that had sat empty in my husband's office. When my husband asked me about it, he was not in agreement that it should have been given away. I apologized and contacted my mother to get it back. She kindly understood, and it's back in our home. By the way, we did put it to use after doing some rearranging. Restitution benefits both parties. The person receiving the recompense no longer has a grievance, and the one making restitution no longer has guilt. Case closed.

Heeding Reproof brings us back to Fear of the LORD, Instruction, Knowledge, Understanding, Discretion, and Counsel.

Welcome to Wisdom's house, the house of the Seven Pillars.

Further Study for Reproof

1. Read 1 Corinthians 3:1–3. What Reproof did Paul give to the church?

2. Read Galatians 2:11–16. What Reproof did Paul give Peter?

3. Read Revelation 2:12–16. The church in Pergamos was given Reproof for allowing what two false doctrines?

4. Read Matthew 18:15–17. What are the steps for church discipline?

Answer Keys for Further Study Sections

Further Study Answers for Fear of the LORD

1. We are to fear the LORD our God for our good always.

2. According to Job 28:28, wisdom is the fear of the LORD.

3. "The fear of the LORD is clean, enduring for ever." (Psalm 19:9a)

4. Pride is described as a foot that steps on others or kicks others out of the way.

5. Arrogancy was evident in the church at Corinth in that the people had divided themselves into

followers of Paul, Apollos, Cephas, or Christ. Each division thought it was better than the others.

6. Diotrephes was following the Evil Way because he spoke against the authority of the apostles and would not receive visiting brethren.

7. The expression "be cut out" means "to be stopped; will come to an end."

8. The Lord will bless the house of Israel, the house of Aaron, and those who fear the LORD.

Further Study Answers for Instruction

1. a. The instructor was Jehoiada the priest. b. The one taught was Jehoash, king of Judah. c. The Instruction was that which was right in the sight of the Lord; God's Law.

2. a. The three instructors were Asaph, Jeduthun, and Heman. b. The Instruction was learning to play and sing songs of the Lord. c. The total number of those instructed was 288.

3. a. The instructors were his grandmother Lois and his mother Eunice. b. The one taught was Timothy. c. The Instruction was learning the Holy Scriptures.

4. a. The instructor had been Hananiah the prophet. b. The Jews had been taught. c. Rebellion against the Lord had been taught. d. Hananiah died that year.

5. a. The instructor was Jesus. b. The ones being taught were His disciples. c. The Instruction was His coming crucifixion and resurrection. d. They didn't ask for an explanation, because they were afraid to ask Him.

Author's Note: If Instruction is not clear to us, we should not let fear hinder us from asking questions.

Further Study Answers for Knowledge

1. a. Abraham used the name Jehovah-Jireh. b. God provided Himself a ram for a sacrifice in the place of Isaac.

2. a. The waters at Marah were bitter. b. The bitter waters were made sweet when Moses by God's command threw in a particular tree.

3. a. The enemy was Amalek. b. The Lord would fight for Israel.

4. Jabal dwelt in tents and raised cattle.

5. Jubal invented the harp and organ.

6. The metals Tubal-Cain used were brass and iron.

7. Man before the flood was intelligent and creative (smart from the start).

8. The Ten Commandments
    I. Thou shalt have <u>no</u> other gods <u>before</u> me.
    II. Thou shalt not <u>make</u> thee any <u>graven</u> <u>image</u>.
    III. Thou shalt not take the <u>name</u> of the LORD thy God in <u>vain</u>.
    IV. Remember the <u>sabbath</u> day, to keep it <u>holy</u>.
    V. <u>Honour</u> thy father and thy mother.
    VI. Thou shalt not <u>kill</u>.
    VII. Thou shalt not commit <u>adultery</u>.
    VIII. Thou shalt not <u>steal</u>.
    IX. Thou shalt not bear <u>false</u> <u>witness</u>.
    X. Thou shalt not <u>covet</u>.

9. God's Word is described as a two-edged sword.

10. We are to meditate on God's Word day and night.

Further Study Answers for Understanding

1. We gain Understanding through God's precepts.

2. We can learn God's commandments from Understanding.

3. We can know God's testimonies from Understanding.

4. The simple can get Understanding.

5. The psalmist said that he would live when he was given Understanding.

6. When he was given Understanding, the psalmist promised he would keep God's Law and observe it with his whole heart.

Further Study Answers for Discretion

1. Discretion in Proverbs 11:22 is teaching us that having beauty without intelligence, under-standing, or judgment is ridiculous. It's the very

attractive woman who is simple and knows nothing. Comedies poke fun at this kind of woman.

2. Discretion in Proverbs 19:11 is teaching us that having knowledge, sense, and wisdom will delay or postpone anger. For example, a child knocks over a glass of water at a restaurant and his father starts to feel angry over the child's clumsiness. He then remembers that spills do happen even at restaurants and calms down. Displaying anger would do far more damage than a spill.

3. Discretion in Jeremiah 10:12 teaches us that God in His skillfulness and wisdom created the expanses of the universe. He stretched out the heavens and set in place innumerable stars.

Further Study Answers for Counsel

1. The counsel of the ungodly is not to be followed.

2. Adonijah decided on his own to reign.

3. Nathan gave counsel to Bathsheba because her life and Solomon's life were in danger.

4. Nathan's counsel was for Bathsheba to let David know that Adonijah had declared himself king even though David had chosen Solomon to be king.

5. Sheba hid in the city of Abel.

6. A wise woman confronted Joab about the reason for the siege.

7. It was said in old time, "They shall surely ask counsel at Abel: and so they ended the matter." (II Samuel 20:18) Author's Note: *They ended the matter* refers to the wise people at Abel.

8. In her wisdom, her counsel was that Sheba be beheaded and his head thrown over the wall.

9. The Lord shall guide me with His counsel.

Further Study Answers for Reproof

1. The reproof that Paul gave to the church at Corinth was confronting them about being carnal: there was envying, strife, and divisions.

2. The reproof that Paul gave to Peter was confronting his hypocrisy. Peter had eaten with Gentiles until Jews from Jerusalem came, then Peter separated from the Gentiles in accordance to Old Testament law. Paul reminded Peter that *man is not justified by works of the law, but by the faith of Jesus Christ.* (Galatians 2:16a)

3. The two false doctrines were the doctrines of Balaam and of the Nicolaitanes.

4. The first confrontation is between the trespasser and the offended. If there is no correction, the second confrontation includes one or two more church members. If still no correction, the matter is brought before the church. If still no correction, the trespasser is to be as a heathen man and a publican.

Notes

1. James Strong, *The Exhaustive Concordance of the Bible* (Iowa City: World Bible Publishers, 1989), 445.
2. Editors, *Family Word Finder* (Pleasantville: The Reader's Digest Association, Inc., 1975), 254.
3. "Scientists' Quotes About Evolution," https://creationtoday.org
4. "Scientists' Quotes About Evolution," https://creationtoday.org
5. Editors, *Webster's New Collegiate Dictionary* (Springfield: G. & C. Merriam C., 1951), 49.
6. Curtis Hutson, *Punch Lines* (Murfreesboro: Sword of the Lord Publishers, 1989), 110.
7. James Strong, *The Exhaustive Concordance of the Bible* (Iowa City: World Bible Publishers, 1989), 945.
8. Strong, *The Exhaustive Concordance of the Bible*, p. 310.

9. Strong, *The Exhaustive Concordance of the Bible*, p. 787.

10. Strong, *The Exhaustive Concordance of the Bible*, p. 376.

11. Strong, *The Exhaustive Concordance of the Bible*, p. 830.

12. Strong, *The Exhaustive Concordance of the Bible*, p. 969.

13. Strong, *The Exhaustive Concordance of the Bible*, p. 129.

14. Strong, *The Exhaustive Concordance of the Bible*, p. 397.

15. Nathan J. Stone, *Names of God in the Old Testament* (Chicago: Moody Press, 1944), p. 33.

16. Stone, *The Names of God in the Old Testament*, p. 19–20.

17. Strong, *The Exhaustive Concordance of the Bible*, p. 17

18. Strong, *The Exhaustive Concordance of the Bible*, p. 312

19. Strong, *The Exhaustive Concordance of the Bible*, p. 282.

20. Strong, *The Exhaustive Concordance of the Bible*, p. 558.

21. Strong, *The Exhaustive Concordance of the Bible*, p. 93

22. Strong, *The Exhaustive Concordance of the Bible,* p. 516.

23. Strong, *The Exhaustive Concordance of the Bible,* p. 1075.

24. Strong, *The Exhaustive Concordance of the Bible,* p. 1073.

25. "Origin and meaning of virtue", https://www.etymonline.com

26. Strong, *The Exhaustive Concordance of the Bible,* p. 1001.

27. Strong, *The Exhaustive Concordance of the Bible,* p. 775.

28. Strong, *The Exhaustive Concordance of the Bible,* p. 181

29. Nathan J. Stone, *Names of God in the Old Testament* (Chicago: Moody Press, 1944), 63.

30. Stone, *Names of God in the Old Testament,* 71.

31. Stone, *Names of God in the Old Testament,* 83.

32. "21 George Washington Carver Quotes," https://www.christianquotes.info

33. "Archimedes' Principle – Physics," https://physics.weber.edu

34. Strong, *The Exhaustive Concordance of the Bible,* p. 267.

35. Strong, *The Exhaustive Concordance of the Bible,* p. 267.

36. "Philippians 2 (KJV)," https://www.blueletterbible.org

37. "Philippians 2 (KJV)," https://www.blueletterbible.org

38. "Galatians 5 (KJV)," https://www.blueletterbible.org

39. James Strong, *The Exhaustive Concordance of the Bible* (World Bible Publishers, 1989), 267.

40. Strong, *The Exhaustive Concordance of the Bible*, p. 267.

41. Strong, *The Exhaustive Concordance of the Bible*, p. 251

42. Strong, *The Exhaustive Concordance of the Bible*, p. 267.

43. Sharon Revello, Text message to author, October 2, 2017.

44. Strong, *The Exhaustive Concordance of the Bible*, p. 558.

45. Editors, *Family Word Finder* (Pleasantville: The Reader's Digest Association, Inc., 1975), p. 888.

46. "Titanic Captain Edward Smith Unsinkable Titanic Quotes," Google.

47. Strong, *The Exhaustive Concordance of the Bible*, p. 839.

48. Strong, *The Exhaustive Concordance of the Bible*, p. 182.

49. Strong, *The Exhaustive Concordance of the Bible*, p. 838.
50. Strong, *The Exhaustive Concordance of the Bible*, p. 153.
51. Strong, *The Exhaustive Concordance of the Bible*, p. 841.

About the Author

---✝---

Nancy Sari grew up on a family farm in Upstate New York. After graduating from a secular college, she attended Bible college to further her knowledge of God's Word. She and her husband Anthony, a retired Baptist preacher, have been married thirty-four years and live in Spencer, Wisconsin. God has blessed them with seven children and four grandchildren. She is caregiver to her older brother who lives with them. A veteran home educator, Mrs. Sari enjoys reading, crocheting, celebrating occasions, and seeing God do great things like saving an atheistic grandfather. Her life's motto is "Blessed are the flexible for they shall never be bent out of shape."

CPSIA information can be obtained
at www.ICGtesting.com
Printed in the USA
BVHW042303130722
641927BV00030B/191

9 781630 502782